The Theming of America

THE THEMING OF AMERICA

*Dreams, Visions,
and Commercial Spaces*

Mark Gottdiener

WestviewPress
A Division of HarperCollins*Publishers*

Copyright © 1997 by Westview Press, A Division of HarperCollins Publishers, Inc.

Published in 1997 in the United States of America by Westview Press, 5500 Central Avenue, Boulder, Colorado 80301-2877, and in the United Kingdom by Westview Press, 12 Hid's Copse Road, Cumnor Hill, Oxford OX2 9JJ

Library of Congress Cataloging-in-Publication Data
Gottdiener, Mark.
  The theming of America : dreams, visions, and commercial spaces /
Mark Gottdiener.
    p.   cm.
  Includes bibliographical references and index.
  ISBN 0-8133-3188-9 (hc). — ISBN 0-8133-3189-7 (pbk.)
    1. Architecture—Environmental aspects—United States.
2. Architecture—United States—Themes, motives. I. Title.
NA2542.35.G68   1997
720´.47—dc20   96-38569
                                                                                     CIP

The paper used in this publication meets the requirements of the American National Standard for Permanence of Paper for Printed Library Materials Z39. 48-1984.

10   9   8   7   6   5   4   3   2   1

Contents

Looking at
Themed Environments

The Increasing Use of Themes in Everyday Life

Since the end of World War II, our everyday environment has been altered in profound ways. Before the 1950s there was a clear distinction between the city and the country (Williams 1973). Cities grew as compact, dense industrial environments usually laid out along right-angled grid lines. They possessed a central sector of office towers and an adjacent area of factories tied to rail spurs and roads. Residential areas comprised the classic contrast of the "gold coast and slum." Wealthy, privileged areas of housing were juxtaposed in close proximity with the more modest, sometimes squalid, neighborhoods of industrial workers. Lying in contrast directly beyond the limits of the city was the country—the fields of farm lands, wooded acres and occasional houses of families separated by open space. Cultural styles of life that were either urban (urbane) or rural reflected this dichotomy of land uses as did depictions of city and country dwellers in novels and films (see Redfield 1947).

Beginning with the 1950s the trend toward suburbanization, which had been operating in the United States for over 100 years, began to accelerate and break down the urban/rural dichotomy. Between 1950 and 1970 the plurality of the U.S. population took up residence in the new space created by the large-scale housing development of rural land next to our biggest cities. Decades of suburban growth eradicated the clear distinction between the city and the country, although its vestiges continue to echo in the popular media. Novels and films, for example, are still produced that focus exclusively on cities. They give the impression that the cities are somehow isolated from both the surrounding suburban region and the global forces that influence virtually all places on the earth.

Along with these population shifts, people changed the ways they imputed meaning to their daily environment. Before the 1950s, fundamental

1

class differences between capitalists and workers organized the land use of the industrial city. Neighborhoods, for example, were working class and the local community reflected ethnic, racial and religious solidarity dedicated to the task of raising families. The center of the city, in contrast, belonged to business. During this period the symbols that provided meaning to daily life were quite limited and *understated.* Buildings reflected their functions with a minimum of symbolic trappings. People in neighborhoods signified their culture through the sometimes subtle markings of churches and store signs, often using foreign languages. Symbols of these kinds gave the ethnic enclaves their distinctive style.

After the 1950s, a new theme emerged in the burgeoning spaces of suburbia. People moving to these areas abandoned religious and ethnic markers characteristic of the inner city, replacing them with signs of prestige centering on the status of home ownership. For over a century a residence outside the city signified high status (Veblen 1899). Until the 1950s, this social position was reserved almost exclusively for the wealthiest people who could afford the land and construction costs of a custom-made home or estate. Now, suburban status increasingly characterizes the majority of Americans and the single-family house is our principal sign of prestige. The present-day suburban home is vested with a host of status symbols that anchor daily life in a culture of affluence. Two- or three-car garages, expansive front lawns, separate eating and family rooms, and extensive square footage are just a few of these structural features that also signify prestige.

In sum, the urban environment of the nineteenth and early twentieth centuries was marked by limited thematic content. Symbols were used almost exclusively to denote ethnic enclaves or religious institutions and the business function of buildings. The thematic differentiation of the built environment increased during the turn of the century because of the popularity of suburbanization among the wealthy, who established the norm of prestige associated with their country estates. Most of the symbolic activity at the time, therefore, involved designating class or ethnic status as the major social markers of the population.

Since the 1960s, a new trend of symbolic differentiation within the built environment has appeared that contrasts graphically with the earlier period. More frequent use of symbols and motifs characterizes the space of everyday life in both the city and the suburb. Signification involves not only a differentiation of particular material objects, but also a constant reworking of facades and interior spaces by overarching motifs drawing on a broad range of symbols. These new modes of thematic representation organize daily life in an increasing variety of ways. Social activities have moved beyond the symbolic work of designating ethnic, religious or affluent status to an expanding repertoire of meanings. More important, and in contrast to previous historical periods, today's environmental symbolism is derived from our popular culture—from common themes that can also be found in films, popular music and novels. In turn, today's themed environments constitute, in fact, a part of our popular culture as well. Consequently, while symbolic elements were muted in the settlement spaces of the early 20th century, construction of metropolitan places today reverses that trend. Our present themed environment merges fluidly with contemporary, commercialized popular culture and the entertainment media.

The Shift to a Themed Environment

Whether people live in the central city or suburbs, themed experiences increasingly characterize their daily life. People eat lunches and dinners in restaurants that compete with each other for the most attractive motifs. These include the signature logos of McDonald's, Burger King, and the like in the franchised world of fast foods; smaller-scaled theme restaurants that cater to particular tastes, such as Chi-Chi's for Mexican-style food, the Olive Garden for Italian-style franchise cooking, and The Red Lobster for seafood; or more elaborately themed environments, such as the Hard Rock Cafe and Planet Hollywood, that draw on the aura of celebrity in films and rock music. Finally, individually owned restaurants tout their personal themes as they struggle for business in the competitive world of dining out, by adding to the density or variety of symbolic decor.

Motifs are also increasingly used to organize recreational activities in both central cities and suburbs. Professional sports, with their aggressive merchandising and team boosterism, offer themed experiences that focus almost as much on abstract symbols worn as clothing or sold as poster images as on the spectacular players of the game. The motifs of teams and sports figures are found on shoes, jackets, hats, and even men's suits. Family entertainment often involves visits to theme parks or themed attractions. Disneyland in California and Disneyworld in Florida are, perhaps, the most famous of these. However, the creation of theme parks for family vacations is increasingly popular throughout the country. Dolly Parton, the country and western singer, has her own park (Dollywood), as does the dead Elvis (Graceland)—both in Tennessee. Las Vegas, once a mecca for alcohol, sex, and gambling, has become the theme park capital of the United States as casinos switch to family oriented entertainment and spectacular fantasy facades, such as the Luxor Hotel with its ancient Egypt motif.

Nature, itself, is not immune from this transformation to motifs. Government regulation and construction redesign have worked over natural wonders, such as Niagara Falls on the New York-Canadian border and the Grand Canyon National Park in Arizona, to heighten the theme of mother nature in an idealized sense. There is still considerable debate over just how much intervention should be allowed in national parks like Yellowstone.

Around the globe, however, there is hardly a pristine area left that hasn't been the subject of some government regulation or human resculpting to fit the needs of commercial interests.

The forms of a symbol-ridden environment pervade everyday life as our material milieu blends its images with those of commercial advertising, television, films, and music. Shopping increasingly occurs in large suburban malls or special central-city districts that use defined themes to entice consumers. Architecture and decor artfully play out distinctive symbolic appeals that connect the mall shopping experience with the media world of television, advertising, and fashion. Finally, the idea of a single, overarching theme has recently been incorporated into the construction of museums and historical monuments. The Holocaust Museum in Washington, D.C., for example, orchestrates the visitor experience entirely around the theme of Germany's failed destruction of European Jewry during World War II. The government also recently converted its abandoned immigrant absorption center on Ellis Island, in New York City harbor, to a popular tourist attraction using a themed milieu. The latter documents the immigration experience to the United States. This motif is painstakingly developed and highlighted in the restored buildings of the former absorption center. Additionally, almost every city in the United States has some version of a national monument, immigrant historical site or war memorial. These not only commemorate some event or experience of history, but also play a fundamental role in the active competition for tourist dollars and corporate investment through the creation of attractive, popular city sites, such as the new Rock and Roll Hall of Fame in Cleveland, Ohio, designed by I. M. Pei.

In sum, the themed milieu with its pervasive use of media culture motifs that define an entire built space increasingly characterizes not only cities but also suburban areas, shopping places, airports, recreation spaces such as baseball stadia, museums, restaurants, and amusement parks. Progressively, then, our daily life occurs within a material environment that is dependent on and organized around overarching symbols, many of which are clearly tied to commercial enterprises. This book explores the nature of this social change as it has developed since the 1960s, the reasons for its emergence, its connections to the economy, and its development as a new cultural form of varied thematic appeals.

Understanding Themed Environments

When I refer to a themed environment I mean the material product of two social processes. First, attention is directed quite literally to environments, that is, to large material forms that are socially constructed which serve as containers for human interaction. These milieus are social spaces within which the public can mingle. Second, themed material forms are also products of a cultural production process that seeks to use constructed spaces as symbols. The latter, then, *convey* meaning to inhabitants. On the receiving side of this relation—regarding the inhabitants or users of these themed spaces—interpretation of symbols takes on a range of meanings according to the reaction of people when exposed to symbolic motifs. The range of responses can include everything from no response at all (that is, a failure of the symbolic content to stimulate), to a variety of reactions dependent on individual associations invoked by the environment, to a negative response, and even displeasure. Thus, I do not suggest that themed environments automatically provoke desire and pleasure from its users. At times such spaces can be the source of great irritation, such as in the strong negative reaction to a poorly designed building. However, the predominant content of our present themed environment derives from highly popular commercial images associated with television, advertising, films, and popular music such as country or rock. It is the latter melding of material forms and commercial culture that characterizes the present from previous historical periods which also used symbolic motifs in their environments.

Another important distinction concerns the way I use the concepts "production" and "consumption." The former refers to a *social* process of creation often involving a group of individuals brought together within an organized, institutional context, such as real estate development. Consumption involves the way individuals or groups *use* or interpret the constructed space by imputing some meaning or meanings to it that guide their behavior. Users may be customers, inhabitants, visitors, or clients, but they are all users of the space in some fashion. Consumption of a themed environment refers to this experience of individuals within a themed milieu, including the assumption of a particular orientation to space based on the personal or group interpretation of its symbolic content. Thus, built forms have the power to alter human behavior through meaning, and this response is also part of what I mean by the process of consumption in space.

Visitors to a themed park will consume the environment itself, besides the rides and attractions. In fact, they have to pay a price of admission before they can enter the park. Within the theme park, they adjust their behavior according to the stimuli received from the signals embedded in built forms. Motifs and symbols developed through the medium of the park's material forms may be highly stimulating, or, conversely, they may hardly be noticed at all. Always, however, individual or group presence in the themed space and the use by people of constructed locations to satisfy specific needs such as food, recreation, communion, or entertainment constitutes what I mean by the "consumption" of the material environment.

In what follows I shall discuss both the production and the consumption of themed milieus. Most commentaries on places like Disneyland, for example, ignore the intentions behind the production of the park and their role in the creation of meaning through environmental means. Instead, they focus exclusively on impressionistic accounts of a visit there. The emphasis seems to be solely on how individuals behave in a particular place or on what those places "mean" from the point of view of the writer. The discussions to follow will seek to correct this one-sided view by emphasizing the process of production of themed environments and their purpose or role in the larger economic organization of our society. I am especially interested in the intermixing of creation and use; that is, how milieus designed for profit interact with the dreams, fantasies, and forms of popular entertainment for people in our society.

Production in Consumption

Despite the dichotomization of the inter-related concepts of production and consumption, there is a less sharp distinction between these two social processes than I have suggested above. To begin with, as our society progressively shifts from an economy dependent on manufacturing to one that is specialized in service industries, the number and types of jobs held by the bulk of the population are increasingly associated with thematic experiences. Museum exhibits, for example, more frequently concern the elaboration of themes than in the past; employees in restaurants and recreational areas are required to conform to the symbolic decor by wearing costumes, and retailing activity increasingly locates in motific milieus such as malls. Thus, the world of work, or production, penetrates and merges with the world of consumption.

Second, it has become harder to isolate the activity of shopping or leisure pursuits as an act of consumption alone. In the past, observers of mass cultural participation often did just that by painting the users or the audience as a group of *passive* consumers conditioned by advertising to behave according to the way producers wished. More recently, analysts of culture recognize that the gross manipulation of people by advertising is an exaggeration. Instead, we must acknowledge the relative autonomy of individuals in the act of consumption as they blend personal history, the self-actualization of their identities, group pressures of various kinds, and the powerful compulsions of the consumer society that pressure people to make certain choices in the marketplace.

As individual identities become wrapped in modes of self-expression and the fashioning of particular lifestyles in response to the great variety of market choices, there is a blurred line between production and consumption. More and more, we view the pursuit of particular styles of life and the development of contemporary subjectivities through the use of material objects as a form of production itself (de Certeau 1984; Gergen 1991). There is always an element of production in the act of consumption, just as there is also a corresponding aspect of use-value exploited by the production process. These intersecting, liminal activities of the economy are increasingly organized by the large, themed commercial milieus comprising today's built environment. In short, people are not like the passive, media-manipulated masses often depicted by analysts of advertising. They are very often proactive in their attitude toward commodities and shopping. Through the daily use of strategies, they "produce" an attitude and a strategy of coping behavior in their social role as consumer.

Another way of viewing the links between the processes of production and consumption focuses on the development of subjectivity and the emergence of the self within a consumer-oriented society (see Langman 1992; Gergen 1991). To be sure, images and desires produced by the advertising industry constantly prime people to consume. When they enter the commercial realms of consumption, as in a visit to a mall, the themed retailing environment actualizes their *consumer selves*. This process, however, is not a passive one with individuals acting as marionettes pulled back and forth by powerful consumer conditioning. Instead, they *self-actualize* within the commercial milieu by seeking through the market ways of satisfying desires and pursuing personal fulfillment that express deeply-held images of the self. Granted, mass advertising conditions much of this actualization of a consumer identity, especially aided by the group force of conformity to fashion. Equally valid is the observation that self-actualization is destined to be disappointed in the alienated world of mass marketing. However, the fashioning of consumer identities is a lot less controlled by advertising manipulation than is often supposed, and the incredibly prolific abundance of commercial products does promise the satisfaction of many of our desires, whether these are manufactured for us or not.

A third and final way of illustrating the interrelatedness between production and consumption involves the changing nature of themed milieus. Today's commercial environments are not only increasingly themed, they are also entertaining. People are not merely passive consumers of goods and services that are offered by such spaces, they also derive enjoyment from their presence in motific milieus. Many environments are designed specifically to entertain. They include theme parks and very large malls, like the Edmonton Mall in Canada, which features indoor swimming, or the indoor arena in Tokyo, Japan, which features skiing. Places compete with each other by promoting entertaining experiences while other activities are stimulated, such as shopping, dining, recreation, and even education (in visits to museums). The creation of entertaining environments that are based on popular culture symbols increasingly characterizes the material forms of our society.

To illustrate these aspects of production in consumption, consider the activity of dressing in daily life. Group norms have always regulated socially acceptable dress (Gottdiener 1994). The large fashion industry orchestrates modes of appearance in modern society and, lately, targets men as well as women for both periodic changes and the production of desire. Despite the power of fashion, most individuals hold a very personalized conception of their dress patterns. They often seek self-actualization and pursue certain distinct lifestyles through the medium of appearance (see Stone 1962; Simmel 1957; Konig 1973). People in our society spend a great deal of money on clothing—more than they could possibly need for purely protective purposes. Yet, they use these material objects in many ways to exploit social situations for their own advantage. Individuals may "dress for success" or to impress; they may seek approval of others—women, men, prospective in-laws, a possible employer; they often seek identification with particular groups by dressing like them; finally, people often mix and match objects of clothing and accessories daily in a *creative* effort to fashion a personal look or image. When considering the social process of dress, then, as distinct from fashion dictated by the clothing industry, it becomes difficult to separate aspects of production and consumption because the two are so interrelated in the daily behavior of dressing (see Barthes 1983).

A Brief Introduction to Semiotics

In the opening section of this chapter we have already begun to use concepts associated with the analysis of symbols in specific ways. This is necessary to discuss the phenomenon of the themed environment in comprehensive detail. Consequently, another feature of this book is its use of semiotics to examine the role of themes in social life. The subject of semiotics, an inquiry started around the turn of the century, concerns itself with aspects of meaning production and consumption as a function of social processes (see Barthes 1967, 1972; Eco 1976; Peirce 1931; de Saussure 1966; Baudrillard 1983; Hervey 1982; Greimas 1966, 1972; Gottdiener 1995). This field and its concepts are useful for the analysis of symbols in the themed environments that are increasingly characteristic of our society.

The basic unit of semiotics is the *sign* defined conceptually as something that stands for something else, and, more technically, as a spoken or written word, a drawn figure, or a material object unified in the mind with a particular cultural concept. The sign is this unity of a word-object, known as a *signifier*, with a corresponding, culturally prescribed concept or meaning, known as a *signified*. Thus our minds attach the word "dog," or the drawn figure of a "dog," as a signifier to the idea of a "dog," that is, a domesticated canine species possessing certain behavioral characteristics. If we came from a culture that did not possess dogs in daily life, however unlikely, we would not know what the signifier "dog" means.

This book takes for its subject the articulation between cultural symbols and material objects that are environments and the relevance of these "themed milieus" to current social processes. Using the concepts of semiotics I can now be more specific. When dealing with objects that are signifiers of certain concepts, cultural meanings, or ideologies of belief, we can consider them not only as "signs," but *sign vehicles*. Signifying objects carry meanings with them. They may purposefully be constructed to convey meaning. Thus, Disneyland, as a theme park, is a large sign-vehicle of the Disney ideology. This concept, however, has two aspects that are often a source of confusion. When we use a signifier to convey simple information, usually of a functional nature, we *denote* meaning. The word train, for example, denotes a mode of transportation or movement. Objects that denote a particular function are called *sign-functions*. Every material form within a given culture is a sign of its function and denotes its use. When we approach a building that is a bank, we understand its meaning at the denotative level in terms of its sign-function as a repository and transaction space for money.

Every signifier, every meaningful object, in addition, conveys another meaning that exists at the *connotative* level; that is, it *connotes* some association defined by social context and social process beyond its denotative sign function. The word "train," which denotes transportation, also connotes old-fashioned travel, perhaps "the 19th century" by association, maybe a sort of romanticism of traveling, mystery, exoticism, and intrigue as in the Orient Express, or in another vein, slowness, noise, pollution, and crowds. The bank building, which is the sign-function for the activity of "banking" also *connotes* a variety of socially ascribed associations including wealth, power, success, future prospects, college educations for our children, and savings for vacations or Christmas. In short, while every sign denotes some social function and conveys a social meaning at the denotative level, each also connotes a variety of associations that have meanings within specific cultural contexts. Thus, sign-vehicles that are material objects operate on *many* social levels.

Understanding the dual nature of signs provides an appreciation for the rich cultural life of objects. It also means that we can understand how material objects are used as signs in social interaction. Rather than considering objects as signs, that is, as existing exclusively in the mind of the interpreter, we also consider signs as objects, as material forms that are used and manipulated by social process, especially advertising. On the one hand, we experience signs as objects, as material forms, when we visit a theme park. On the other hand, social activities convert objects into signs in order for them to function properly. Both processes operate simultaneously, depending on the point of reference.

Because signs perform double duty in social interaction (denoting and connoting), their interpretation is fraught with ambiguity. Furthermore, individuals decoding signs use their personal frame of reference, unless taught not to. This may lead to the interpretation of a particular sign or discourse that was unintended by its producer, who may have come from another social context. For these reasons, the meaning attached to signs is always *polysemic*, that is, there are always several equally valid ways of interpreting a sign. Due to the presence of polysemy, the understanding of meaningful interaction is always problematic. Communication between individuals is a difficult rather than easy task, especially because the *interpretation* of communication invariably differs from person to person, even within the same receiving context. Understanding polysemy and its effects is a major enterprise of semiotics. Recognizing cases of polysemy is also an important aspect of the interpretation of signs.

Despite the polysemic interpretation of signs by different individuals, social forces of control work through language and communication media to constrain the use of words or images to a specific universe of meaning. Where would commodity producers motivated by profit be without advertising? What would politicians or film stars do without professional publicity agents? The pursuit of both profit and public office in corporate America is achieved by a media culture that manipulates the audience for desired ends while it purports to entertain us all. Therefore, in addition to the property of any sign system to allow many synonyms for each concept, the social activities of speech, writing, and image production depend on the ability of modes of communication to convey intended meanings.

Powerful interests in society, such as corporate business leaders or officials of government, accomplish the task of manipulating the public towards their desired ends by constraining the normally wide range of meanings in social discourse. One of the most important means of accomplishing this task is through the control of interpretations for images and signs. The key to interpretative frameworks is known in semiotics as *the code*. Thus, powerful interests control the meaning of things by propagating codes that constrain the interpretation of symbols in desired ways. But codes are also the way all of us interpret the signs in our environment and ascribe social meanings to events, emotions, and objects.

A *code* is the *overarching* mode of sign organization that provides the social and cultural context for the "correct" or widely accepted interpretation of specific symbols. Sometimes we also use "*semantic field*" or "*the universe of meaning*" for the concept of code. Its most important characteristic is that it is a subcultural phenomenon shared by others knowledgeable about social context. As Eco (1976) observes, for example, if I say "bachelor," you would understand this word as "male seal" only if we were discussing marine biology and the particular subphylum of sea mammals belonging to Pinnipedia. Our understanding of all communication, all sign systems, relies on our internalization of the appropriate cultural codes and our ability to invoke the appropriate semantic field in discourse.

A diverse society contains populations that invoke a variety of subcultural contexts in the process of communication. Simultaneously, powerful forces in society, such as advertising, economics, and politics marshal customs and everyday habits or normative understandings of appropriate behavior, to limit ambiguity and direct activity toward desired ends. Through these commercial and, in some cases, political forces, the interpretation of our environment can be manipulated or controlled. The interpretative codes that are used specifically to legitimate points of view that are supportive of powerful social interests are known as *ideologies*. Ideological codes are also the basis of propaganda, and they function through culture to maintain powerful interests in their positions of control over society. One of our society's most active ideologies is the "norm of consumption" that stimulates people to purchase commodities even if they go into debt and whether or not their purchase satisfies some basic need. In sum, by directing people's interpretation of their environment, ideologies are specific codes that enable powerful business and state interests to manipulate and control the population. The discussions to follow will focus on a particular source of ideology, namely the culture of consumption, and the way normative expectations support the proliferation of themes in commercial spaces.

An Example of Sign Analysis: The Boulderado Hotel

Our tour of semiotic concepts will aid us in analyzing the themed environments of daily life. Let us consider one example in some detail before proceeding with the remainder of this book. Recently, I spent some time in a themed hotel, the Boulderado, in Boulder, Colorado. The name itself links the location of the city of Boulder to the state of Colorado which has certain connotations and associations of its own. As a play on the word, Colorado, the signifier "Boulderado" invokes the culture of the "Old West" or "Wild West" of the United States. The built environment of the hotel exploits the particular motif, "the West," as in "culture of the American West."

The promotional material for the Hotel Boulderado invokes an image that complements but is also at some variance with these initial connotations invoked by the name. In 1909, long after the height of Wild West culture, local business interests built the Boulderado. It was constructed in the high Victorian style as a luxury hotel by the powerful commercial and landed interests of the city who sought to improve the dollar value of the Boulder location. The Boulderado, as a themed environment, functioned as an intentional sign for these interests, which used the image of the hotel to make money. A local spokesperson for the business community in the town stated before the hotel's construction,

We have invested our money in the enterprise because it represents Boulder's greatest need. We shall be glad of returns, but shall be infinitely gladder if we se-

*A brochure from the Hotel Boulderado,
Boulder, Colorado.*

cure a hotel of such beauty of proportions and material and architectural design
that it will stand as a monument to her permanency and pride in her enterprises.
Let it be the hotel beautiful (Hotel Boulderado, "Legend of a Landmark," n.d).

From its inception, then, the Hotel Boulderado was a themed milieu that
denoted luxurious accommodations and connoted status or prestige. As an
object, it also functioned as a sign-vehicle for the pursuit of wealth by local
business interests. By promoting the hotel as a luxurious and attractive ac-
commodation for travelers, economic interests also promoted the town as a

desirable location in competition with other possible destinations in the West. As we shall discover in subsequent chapters, this pattern of promoting a particular place or location in competition with places elsewhere through the use of a themed environment appears frequently and in a variety of contexts.

The Hotel Boulderado went through several cycles of prosperity and decline since first built. Among its most famous guests was Theodore Roosevelt and, in later years, owners exploited the significance of that visit. Today there is a "Teddy Roosevelt American Grille," which serves as the main dining facility that displays pictures of the dead president within its interior and on its advertising. The presence of a restaurant named after President Roosevelt would make little, if any, sense to someone who is unaware of the historical reference. Conversely, the present reference reinforces the ambiance of the hotel as a historical landmark where important activities once took place.

A themed restaurant chain, Concept Restaurants, now owns the hotel and has retained its Victorian decor. The interior features imitation Tiffany lamps in the lobby and rooms, an impressive stained glass ceiling in the lobby, mahogany-stained furniture and wood detailing, turn-of-the-century patterned wall paper, and old-fashioned metal poster beds. Meeting rooms embellish signification further by using names that invoke the Rocky Mountain setting: Columbine, Balsam, Alpine.

The above signifiers exploit associations with the principal themes of the American West at the turn of the century and play up the cultural capital of visits by famous people in history. These signs operate through connotation. Within the interior, however, there also is a denotative sign system that functions much like it does in any hotel. The main entrance, for example, is framed with a red carpet arched over by a large marquee. Upon entering the building visitors can register in a recognizable hotel lobby with a standard front desk. Through experience with using other hotels, customers are easily able to recognize the signs that guide interaction and maneuver successfully through the space of the hotel from registration to room use. In short, the themed hotel uses both denotative and connotative sign systems to function as a commercial enterprise. The same semiotic aspects are found in all other themed environments.

In the past this hotel, as a material object, was used as a means of accumulating wealth for town interests by making their location special. The object used as a sign worked because the theme of Victorian luxury possessed meaning at that time. Now the same object functions in a slightly different capacity. As a sign it is used as an object in the pursuit of profits by a single company. As an object it is also a sign of nostalgia and a representation of the theme of the "Old West." The latter possesses meaning among tourists in our present society.

The hotel, therefore, functions as a sign despite historical change. In the former period it was used to attract people to Boulder because it signified to them a luxurious, special place. Today, few people, if any, would make the trip there simply to stay at this hotel. However, the appeal of nostalgia may influence some tourists to stay at the Boulderado when they are in the area, instead of at competing hotels. As the discussions to follow show, the themed environment is a tool exploited in business competition or place competition, rather than a symbolic milieu constructed for its own sake. We experience the themed environment, therefore, as the intersection of meaning systems and social processes—in this case profit making, tourism, signs of affluence, business or locational competition, and representations of American history through nostalgia—that comfort us with a semblance of culture.

The Plan of the Book

The following chapters seek not only to describe the variety of themed environments of our present society and to explain how they are used, but, also to understand the reasons for their increasing presence. Chapter 2 places the concept of themed environment in historical context. Symbolism once literally saturated early human existence mainly through signs deriving from the codes of nature, cosmology, or religion. Ancient civilizations added to these sources themed environments based on celebrating state power or the grandeur of rulers who were often themselves considered divine.

The era of capitalist industrialization, which began during the latter middle ages of European society, undercut the symbolic basis of the built environment. Through the passage of centuries, cities lost their once-robust symbolic milieus. Denotative sign systems that marked sign-functions dominated the lived environment by the early 20th century, while connotative signifiers were weak, if present at all. Domination of design and planning by modernist principles eradicated developed thematic elements in cities through new construction that avoided symbols and used indexes to manipulate behavior. Chapter 2 traces these changes from ancient times to the present and illustrates how the construction of themed environments has resurfaced in contemporary society.

Chapter 3 analyzes the role of themes in the social processes of contemporary society. It seeks to explain why motifs are more common today. Understanding comes from investigating the dynamics of profit-making and the problems encountered by our capitalist economy in the twentieth century. In this way, a connection between the recent reliance on themed milieus and the problems of a mature economy is made that explains the growing popularity of the former.

Chapter 4 plunges into the examination of various themed environments. I start with those that are found in the immediate context of everyday life, such as themed restaurants and malls, and then progress to the study of gambling casinos and airports. Next I link the development of these mileus to the dynamics of the present economy. This discussion is continued in Chapter 5 by examining the more spectacular examples of theme parks and natural wonder tourist attractions. I then discuss other, more recent, uses of themes by war memorials and museums that are less connected to the economy and more relevant to society's desire for a mode of representation adequate to events and historical circumstances that seem beyond our symbolic abilities. The latter process attempts to represent the "unrepresentable." The final chapters close with a discussion of the types of themes used by our society and the social significance of the current switch to a milieu that relies on the development of motifs. At present, U.S. culture may be creating and recreating its own myths by trying to provide some deeper meaning or symbolic context to our daily lives.

From a Themed to an Anti-Themed Environment: Natural Codes, Ancient Cities, and Modernism

Even in the earliest human societies, everyday life was over endowed with symbolism. We know this from the historical record and artifacts left by the earliest image makers, such as the cave artists of Lascaux, and the use of symbols among the remaining traditional tribal societies. The daily lives of people in tribal societies project a window into the past, and we can surmise that human existence thousands of years ago must have been very similar to the way traditional societies today wrap a symbolic context, as a blanket, around their activities.

From the earliest moments of human consciousness animism evolved as a great naming exercise. Guided by the belief that every object of nature possessed its own animating specter, humans named the spirit of the trees, the rivers, the stones, the mountains, the sun, the rain, and so on. The presence of these spirits was both acknowledged as intervening in the affairs of people and worshipped for their independent power to intervene. The natural world, then, was possessed by the thousand named apparitions that inhabited its many forms (Schama 1995).

The cave paintings at Lascaux, France, are an example of symbolic production by the earliest humans. These representations have much the same purpose as the symbols of today. Photo courtesy of The Bettmann Archive.

Human imputation of meaning to the natural world involved three distinct activities that were all related. Early humans *believed* in the independent life of the spirits of their environment, they developed extended *discourses* that recounted the cosmologies of their spirits, and they produced *artifacts* that objectified their images of the spirits. The meaningful environment of the ancients was produced by the activities of belief, discourse, and materialization, articulating together in the human practice of recognizing and mollifying the power of their respective gods. Over time we have been left not only with the material artifacts of ancient cultures that signify this rather extensive spirit world but, in many cases, with the discourses of ancient cultures that specify legends, tales, and myths.

As several scholars of sagas point out, myths are empowering to those that believe in them. They enable a society to respond to the environment in positive and controlling ways. Legends, for example, encode important forms of knowledge about managing the external environment. They are, thus, the earliest examples of the close connection between knowledge and power. For instance, Eliade (1963) points to the role that myths of *origins* played in the life of ancient societies. Knowledge of beginnings was controlling knowledge. A society dependent on the cultivation of rice would be left assured of a successful harvest only when the shaman of the tribe would visit the newly planted rice fields and intone the myth of rice's worldly creation (see Eliade 1963, Ch. 2). Individuals also empowered themselves by establishing a totemic connection with an animal or plant spirit. The powers of the spirit, such as leaping, running, hiding, and wisdom, were appropriated through the totemic practice. Material objects, such as totemic masks, the wearing of feathers or fur, and tattoo markings, objectified the relation between humans and their natural spirits. Using the practice of naming, early humans reinforced this relation in discourse. People assumed the names of their totems, such as coyote, fox, or bear, for example, "running fox" or "little bear." As in other cases, then, belief, discourse, and material culture melded in the production of a meaningful, or themed, environment.

Scholars also note the many similarities among the myths of the world's cultures (see Jung, 1964). The story of death and rebirth, for example, is quite common to many societies. Figures such as Osiris among the ancient Egyptians, Orpheus for the Greeks, and Christ for Christians personify the myth of death and rebirth. Many of the same cultures also have elaborate festivals marking the winter and spring solstice, that is, the period of decline and renewal in nature. These same periods are marked today by Christmas and Easter. Symbols such as the phoenix bird and the egg figure into myths of lifecycles, as well. Other legends common to most cultures involve a hero who is godlike and omnipotent. Often the mythical hero rises from humble birth to a triumph through the slaying of some monster, or the vanquishing of an evil threat to the society, but then succumbs to the failing of pride or hubris and meets a heroic death. Samson of the ancient Israelites and Achilles from the Greeks share these attributes. The former possessed strength from long hair; the latter had a critical weakness at the heel. Although seemingly godlike, both died when these flaws were discovered. As in other examples, these stories of folk heroes served to empower the people who believed in them.

The conception of the natural world as a *meaningful* or *signifying* place created the earliest instance of the *themed environment* whose dynamics are the subject of this book. During ancient times, everyday life consisted of fully themed spaces where every tree, stone, place, and or individual had a connotative symbol attached to it, as we discussed. There was once little difference between the name of an object or person, and the name of the spirit that resided in that object or person. Later the threefold process of belief, discourse, and material objectification led to the development of increasingly elaborate legends handed down by cultures. Eventually, people systematized these into cosmologies, mythologies, and religions. Following from their ancient origins in animism, the earliest religions, such as those of the Hindus, Chinese, and Greeks, were pantheistic. A group of gods, who often competed or conspired among themselves, ruled the world, including all animal and plant spirits and humanity. For example, the ancient Greeks believed in the god Pan, who was lord over the woodlands or forests and their spirits; the god Poseidon, lord of the sea; and Cronus or Zeus, who were supreme gods of the earth.

Greek mythology, which was a unified system of belief for the ancient Hellenic and Hellenistic civilizations and which was later adopted by Roman civilization, was already more developed than the animism of primitive traditional societies. Ancient Greeks believed in the gods Apollo and Artemis, who not only ruled natural objects like the sun and the moon respectively, as in animistic cultures, but also human attributes. Apollo, the sun god, was also the god of music, poetry, eloquence, medicine, and the fine arts; Artemis, known by the Romans as Diana, was goddess of the moon but also of the hunt and maidenhood. Athena was one of several divinities that ruled solely over the domain of people. She was the goddess of wisdom, the industrial arts, and war.

In these and other examples, we can observe the development from the spirit naming of the natural environment by primitive societies to the more sophisticated naming of both the natural and human interactive environments in the sacred beliefs of ancient civilizations. This shift involved the development of cosmologies into organized religions based on the pantheon of gods complete with specialized niches in the social division of labor for priests, priestesses, oracles, temple virgins, shamans, seers, and assorted "holy men."

As history unfolded, gods took on more human attributes and humans were more likely to be considered "godlike." The Greek gods quarreled with, were fickle to, and were jealous of each other, behaving as many humans do. Zeus was well known for his sexual trysts with young women like Danaë and Lida. As time went on the role of gods in human interaction increased while their reign over nature became less important. When the Romans adopted Greek mythology as their official religion, they added to the Greek pantheon several additional gods, like Mercury, whose concern was the control of human activities. Eventually, certain Romans such as the Caesars, and other emperors became gods, a redefinition of human ruler to divinity that would never have happened among the Greeks, even though the latter believed the gods sired earthly creatures, such as Hercules. After the Romans, Christians worshipped Jesus for this reason and they still believe in his divine birth. In these and other examples, the activities of the gods over time shifted from the domain of nature alone to intervention in the behavior and social affairs of people. The shift away from the natural and toward the social world occurred at an early period in recorded history.

Accompanying the development of religion from early animism to organized social systems was the same articulation of belief, discourse, and object-making typical of early forms. Ancient civilizations, such as those of Egypt, Greece, and Rome, possessed elaborate rituals and codified texts that systematized mythology. This discourse regulated daily life. The Judeo-Christian bible, which also influenced the Koran, became the central focus for the organized religions of Judaism, Christianity, and Islam. It is now the basis for the religious beliefs of over half the world's population. The bible, as a codified text reproduced from generation to generation, was not the only discursive component of organized religion.

With Judaism, for example, discussion of the core text produced immense reams of commentaries, such as the Babylonian Talmud, and further elaborations that passed from oral to written culture. Around the core text, as happened for Christianity and Islam as well, arose a host of ancillary beliefs and practices, each with their own themes and material objectifications. Such belief systems thoroughly regulated societies, such as those organized by institutionalized religion. Every object, every action, every moment, every person possessed a symbolic-religious connotation. Thus, societies believing in the early religions, continuing today among traditional or fundamental cultures that remain regulated by orthodoxy, were thoroughly themed environments. Individual members of such cultures existed in a medium saturated by symbolic connotations, or what Luckmann (1967) calls life under the "sacred canopy."

In sum, humans have always been symbol-producing beings and from the earliest times of cave paintings and artifact production, they have endowed their environment with themes and signs that held power. Over time this practice produced elaborate discourses or myths. They were empowering stories that people handed down through the generations and that eventually formed the core of organized religious systems.

Human activity is naturally a signifying activity. That is, humans crave and, therefore, create meaning for their actions and their environment. Symbol production was as basic to everyday life as was the search for food, clothing, and shelter. What is more, this activity of meaning creation and circulation remains a fundamental part of life. In what follows, however, we shall see that the production, quality, and social context of themed environments have changed since ancient times, as has their purpose in daily life.

In the earliest societies symbols served to mark off the realm of the sacred from the profane aspects of the larger environment. As civilizations developed, sign systems were tied to political ideologies of empire building and formal religious systems. Thus, by the time of the classical civilizations of ancient Greece and Rome, signs were already being used by people for specific or *motivated* purposes. Today, signs are also used to propagate political and religious ideologies. But, in addition, our environment is increasingly characterized by systems of signs that seek to motivate consumption and are tied to the pursuit of profit. At the very same time, these sign systems also entertain. It is precisely this confluence of commercialism and entertainment that characterizes the themed environments of our society.

The observation that social life involves the quest for meaning is quite commonplace and one that I will not explore in this discussion. In what follows I shall develop, instead, one aspect of this quest, namely, the extension of meaning production and enjoyment to large-scale material environments by social processes for commercial and entertainment purposes. I am especially interested in those themed environments produced by codes existing outside the domains of religion and cosmology. A temple or mosque is a themed environment that is an extension of the organized religious discourses discussed above. But I am less concerned with such artifacts than with secular manifestations of the desire for meaning objectified in other material forms, such as buildings and theme parks, or the current modes of themed retailing, such as malls or restaurants. It is the latter process, I suggest, that increasingly characterizes our culture.

This assertion, which frames the thesis of this book, is *not*, however, a commonplace one. Not too long ago, as recently as the 1970s, much of our material environment was decidedly devoid of significant connotations. The rise of an entertainment-commercialized themed environment is quite recent. Our cultural artifacts prior to the 1950s did possess meaning but only in an attenuated, highly compartmentalized sense. This book, then, seeks to explain both how and why the new modes of symbolic production that have recently appeared increasingly characterize our culture.

Before proceeding with a discussion of contemporary themed environments, I shall explore some early examples of symbolic production through themed settlement spaces and cities. Later in this chapter I shall discuss the shift, experienced in western industrial society from a themed to an anti-themed environment associated with the "modernist movement" in architecture and design. The remainder of this book will then discuss the revival of the desire for themed milieus, which seems to characterize our society, and the reasons for the present shift to spaces that stimulate consumption while seeking to entertain.

The Contrast Between Ancient and Modernist Cities

The increasing reliance on themed milieus in our built environment is an observation of daily life relevant to post-1950s America. Before that time, for the preceding thirty years, the symbolic dimension in architecture was consciously and purposely squelched. Even going further back, to the nineteenth century, the industrial cities of capitalism had an attenuated symbolic structure compared to the cities of the medieval period in the West and ancient times. Thus, what seems surprising today by contrast, namely, the increasing appearance of themed places in our quotidian environment, was quite common and, in fact, normative for ancient cities. These places, such as Athens, Rome and Beijing during the period of empires, existed as material expressions of cultural themes. All ancient cities were overendowed with built forms that were symbols. The ancient city, itself, was a symbol or symbolic expression both of a particular person's civilization and a material environment that sheltered and contained social activities within a signifying space.

The Ancient City

All ancient civilizations constructed settlement spaces that were overendowed with meaning and material symbols. The place of daily living was itself symbolic as the built environment encapsulated the typical resident in a richly textured, sign-filled space. Even now, many traditional societies retain the importance of signs and overarching themes in the construction of their settlement spaces.

Ancient societies most commonly built places using a cosmological ideology. Buildings were situated according to particular directions that promised luck or paid homage to the gods. The present practice of *fung shuei* by many Chinese people embodies these ancient cosmological practices of siting. They believe that good or ill fortune depends, in part, on the way living spaces are situated in regard to the cosmological axis. A *fung shuei* expert will analyze buildings and houses for a preferred location and proper placement of windows and doors to protect against evil forces and to promote good luck or success. Ancient societies endowed their places with meaningful symbols for these and other reasons, including the quest for fertility, the celebration of the empire, the glorification of rulers and gods, the alignment with nature, and the desire to promote good fortune.

Ancient Athens

Classical Athens was constructed according to a combined cosmological and religious code that both situated the settlement in harmony with nature and endowed its buildings with homages to the gods. The entire city, its environmental space, and its buildings signified through material elements the belief in the pantheon of Greek gods, so that its inhabitants lived within a sacred and meaningful space.

As suggested by its name, Athens was built by the Greeks to honor the goddess Athena. The early Greeks conceived of the world as a circular orbit with a sacred center. Consequently, Athens was planned using the circle as its principal figure. At its center was the sacred public hearth, or the *hestia koine*, which was the center of the community. The Greeks of the 6th century B.C. considered this space as the sacred center of the world, or the *omphalos*, which was also the anchoring point for the cosmological axis of the universe. Surrounding the sacred center was the *agora*, which encapsulated the public hearth and reserved the surrounding space for the central functions of the city, including its civic and political functions, and the central economic institution of the marketplace. Thus, Athenians conducted the ordinary, mundane activities of daily life, such as buying and selling, legal matters and politics, within a circular space that possessed a sacred center symbolizing the community hearth.

An elevated mesa, called the Acropolis, dominated the entire city. On its flat top the Greeks built the finest structure of the ancient world, the Parthenon, a temple dedicated to Athena. As happened with all sacred buildings located throughout the city, the Parthenon was scaled according to the golden mean— a set of proportions dictating width, height, and length believed to order the natural universe and, therefore, to signify the sacred proportions of the cosmos. Because the temple of Athena dominated the Acropolis and because the Acropolis dominated all of Athens, the symbols of its religion, which we now know as Greek mythology, blanketed this ancient city and made it a sacred space. Within the settlement space and constructed according to the sacred proportions of the golden mean, all buildings were endowed with the same cosmological and religious meanings deriving from Greek cosmology.

Ancient Beijing

The chinese emperor transformed the city of Beijing during the European middle ages, that is, about 1500 A.D. At that time the Manchu dynasty picked the city for the capital of its empire. For hundreds of years before this period, Beijing functioned as a city of commerce and business with important trading connections to the rest of the known world. Imperial China was much different from the civilization of the ancient Greeks. Unlike the latter, the Chinese possessed a vast empire ruled by a single individual, the emperor, thousands of years after the height of Athens. His armies and bureaucrats controlled great wealth and immense natural and population resources. Overlaying the cosmological and religious symbols of ancient China, which had their counterparts in Greek civilization, the city of Beijing also symbolized the political power of the monarch, its emperor, and his state. The Manchu dynasty claimed divinity and omniscient power over all the subjects of the kingdom. As a result, a separate system of signs surfaced that dealt with the royal household, its dwellings, and its activities that signified their sacred status.

The city of Beijing during the 1500s A.D., combined both a practical city and the symbolism in select places of Chinese cosmology and religion. The Manchu emperors transformed this space to signify their own power and sacred status. They claimed for themselves the geographic center of the city and erected a symbolic, sacred, and restricted environment in their honor. This so-called Forbidden City contained the Manchu emperor's palace, its fortifications, and within them, the houses where the ruler, his family, his court, and all his close functionaries lived. Every other resident was restricted from entering the boundaries of the Forbidden City under pain of death. This sacred center of Beijing was, for the ordinary resident, an empty space defended against access; in addition to organizing the plan of the city, it also served as a religious symbol that was protected from the profaneness of everyday life.

The emperor's palace and the Forbidden City containing it provided the overarching symbolic structure to the larger space of Beijing. Within the Forbidden City itself, however, additional cosmological and religious symbols articulated with the built environment, providing detailed meanings and signs as part of the construction of buildings. As the French historian, Ferdinand Braudel remarks,

> The heart of the palace was behind the second wall. This was the forbidden city, the Yellow City, where the Emperor lived protected by his guards, by check points at the gates, protocol, ramparts, moats and the vast corner pavilions with twisted roofs, the Kialoleou. Every building, every gate and every bridge had its own name and, as it were, its own customs and practices. The forbidden town measured 1 kilometer by 780 meters (1973:428–429).

Thus, very much like ancient Athens, Beijing possessed both an overarching symbolic structure that provided the entire space with a system of meaning and an individual symbolic structure for the elements of the built environment. These sign systems drew on cosmological/religious codes that articulated with the demands of state power. In both cases, the space of settlement was sacred, although in Beijing's case, sacredness existed on two levels and included the most holy forbidden city at its center.

The Dogon Village

Athens represents a signifying city environment of the sixth century B.C., while Beijing and its Forbidden City were constructed around 1500 A.D. Today there are few comparable places overendowed and overarched by cosmological and/or religious codes. Vatican City, in Italy, is one example. Some interesting signifying spaces at present can be found among traditional societies in the less developed world. One such example is the village of the Dogon located in the southwestern section of the Sudan. (See Figure 2.2.) This settlement space is constructed according to a cosmological code that references both the axes of the world and the male/female counterparts of the people (Lagopoulos, 1986; Griaule, 1966). According to Lagopoulos (1986:264), with regard to the cosmological component,

> The shape of the settlement, according to the Dogon must be elliptic. The main square, according to this model, is located to the north and comprises the council house and the oval altar; the latter is quadrangular in plan and its corners are oriented toward the cardinal points of the compass. The signified of the square ... is the sky and the primordial field. This field is held to be divided into 60 parts, in the image of the earth and of the world.

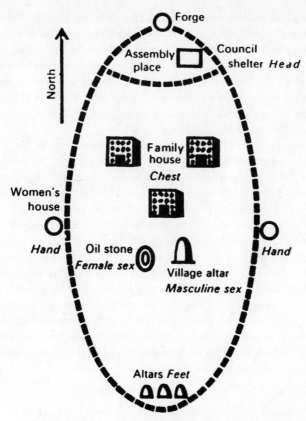

A semiotic rendering of the Dogon Village, Africa.
Reproduced courtesy of Columbia University Press.

With regard to the representation of the body,

> The signified of the council house is a head, while those of the altar are the egg of the creator Amma, the center of the world, and the point of departure of the ... creation. North of the square there is the forge, the signified of which is a mythical forge. At the center of the settlement there is a set of stones, the signified of which is the female genital organ. Respect for women leads to the construction of the foundation altar, having as its signified the male genital organ, outside the settlement, while normally it ought to have stood beside the set of stones already referred to. Two other elements of the settlement have as their signified one hand each, and a third, the legs. The signified of the entire settlement is a man lying flat on his back (1986:264–265).

In short, the more contemporary space of the Dogon village is doubly articulated and, therefore, overendowed with meaning. On the one hand, the spatial array signifies the cosmological axis and the location of the village compared with the cosmos. On the other hand, the settlement space is a representation of the hermaphroditic human body with both male and female genital organs present, that is, the human body without the tension of gender distinctions. The head of this settlement space is also the assembly place of the entire village and the location of the council house. A typical resident of the Dogon village stands physically in a space that provides meaning in both a cosmological and human sense.

A simple comparison between the settlement space of the Dogon and our own "modern" cities reveals how limited is our signifying environment. The contemporary city is superhuman in scale dwarfing our own physical proportions. Siting ignores the cosmological axis of the earth and is dictated by the economics of commercial location and real estate development. Buildings are not constructed with clear symbolic referents in mind. They only signify their function—a bank, school, shopping center, or gas station. In short, whereas the ancient world and the settlement space of traditional society were overendowed with symbols, our cities have for several past centuries of industrial/capitalist development been constructed with attenuated symbolic referents and the rejection of cosmological or religious themes. This transformation from the richly endowed, connotatively signifying space of the ancient and traditional city to the functional, denotative space of modern cities, which is presently being reversed in the themed environment, is the subject of the next section.

Early Modernist Forms in the City: The Transition from a Signifying to an Anti-Signifying Environment

After the Middle Ages, in the industrialized West, built environments underwent a transition to a settlement space with an attenuated symbolic content. Before that time, as we have seen, people built their settlement spaces with clearly defined symbolic referents in mind. Even during the European Middle Ages, people engineered a definitive symbolic content in the design of buildings. Then it was the church that dominated city space. Usually a particular church, if not a large cathedral, became the central focus for the town. After knowledge of the Holy Land circulated back to Europe, people occasionally designed towns according to the crusader maps of Jerusalem. This plan consisted of one long corridor running lengthwise through the city, after the roman *cardo* in Jerusalem, and a second thoroughfare that bisected the main street, so that the entire configuration was in the sign of the cross. They located the most important church or cathedral at the intersection of the two main streets. Thus, the entire ensemble derived a sacred significance through analogy with the city of Jerusalem (Lagopoulos, 1986).

With the coming of capitalism, religion and local signifying practices were pushed aside in favor of the functional need of accumulating wealth. According to Roland Barthes (1986), the classic city of early capitalism grew around a center that contained buildings corresponding to the most powerful forces of social organization. There was a church, a bank or brokerage house, a court or civic building, and a space for a market. Usually the buildings themselves surrounded a large town square, which functioned as a market much in the same way the agora did in ancient Greece.

Besides the church, which retained the symbolic trappings of traditional society, the buildings of the center possessed little in the way of symbolic embellishments. The structures were known best by their functions—a bank, a court, a commercial brokerage. Francoise Choay refers to this attenuation of the power of signs in the early capitalist city as "hyposignification." As she notes, "Hyposignificant does not mean without signification, but only that the built-up system no longer refers to the totality of cultural behavior" (Choay 1986:170). Thus, although most societies retained richly structured symbolic systems of religion and historical tradition, their capitalist downtowns were relatively devoid of meaning and were functionally structured by the needs of business.

Choay (1986: 170) argues that with capitalism came a "semantic reduction," a change to a functional system of meaning in urban space with city buildings limited to symbolizing the role they played in society. A built environment with signs dominated by links to the economic or capital accumulation process overshadowed the richness of traditional and medieval symbolism. In the terminology of semiotics discussed in Chapter 1, this means that buildings lost their religious and cosmological referents and became "sign-functions" of their societal role.

By the late nineteenth-century in the West, urban living had already become problematic and many societal leaders had become appalled at the living and working arrangements of people in the industrial city. The filth and congestion of factories, frequent public health crises, the rapid spread of epidemics, and the increase in poverty, homelessness, and abandoned children were some obvious urban plagues of nineteenth century capitalism. In response to the problems of the hyposignificant, functional city, urban reformers began to dream of alternate environments that also served as critiques of current city living. The new planning models addressed the ills of urban life through utopian planning and, simultaneously, infused the built environment with richer symbolism. In the United States, many of these schemes culminated in organized "world expositions," such as the 1893 Columbian Exposition held by the city of Chicago. These public affairs provided people with alternative visions of daily life and provided both architects and planners with freedom to experiment with new environmental forms.

Choay (1986:242–256) mentions two seminal plans that were critiques of industrial urbanization that appeared at the turn of the last century: the nostalgic and the progressivist models which also informed utopian aspects of American urban expositions. The dream of nineteenth-century utopian planners oriented "itself along the two basic dimensions of time, past and future" (1986:242). In both cases, an attempt was made to withdraw from the functional code of capitalism and return city building to a signifying environment using the more expressive codes of naturalism and progressivism.

The Nostalgic-Culturalist Planning Model

The nostalgic model, also known as the culturalist model, drew upon antiurbanist feelings and a yearning for the close community of past village life. Choay mentions the antiurban writings of early American thinkers as most illustrative of the nostalgic model.

> The large city is thus criticized successively from a series of different angles; in the name of democracy and political empiricism by Jefferson; in the name of a metaphysics of nature by Emerson and mainly by Thoreau; finally, as a function of a simple analysis of human relations by the great novelists. All these writers, in unison, naively place their hopes in the restoration of a kind of *rural* state which they think is compatible, with a few reservations, with the economic development of industrial society and which alone will ensure the safeguarding of liberty, the blossoming of personality and true community (1986:244).

This yearning for the more humane, naturally endowed built environment of the past inspired several alternate visions of city living. Two of the most influential were the "garden city" plans of the Englishman Ebeneezer Howard and the naturalist model of the American architect Frank Lloyd Wright. For Howard, the complete rupture between the urban pavement and the rural countryside was a mistake. On the one hand, the pristine rhythms of nature were forgotten and, on the other, the city, cut off as it was from nature, was free to grow to any size, dwarfing human scale and the ability of people to manage their own society. Howard proposed, instead, a plan for all new city building that strove for a balance between the urban and the rural. Cities would be limited in size, surrounded completely by a circular *green belt* of vegetation, traffic would be restricted to distinct corridors and housing would be airy with easy access to gardens and green areas.

The vision of Frank Lloyd Wright developed during the turn of the last century was very similar to that of Howard's. Society's ills were blamed on the big industrial city. As the poet Emerson had preached, only a return to nature could cure people of the evils of capitalist industrialization. Wright envisioned a new model of building, which he called "Broadacre City."

> Nature here again becomes a continuous environment, in which all the urban functions are **dispersed** and isolated under the form of **limited units**. Housing is individual: not apartments, but private houses with at least four acres of property each, land which the proprietor uses for agriculture and for different leisure activities. Work is sometimes attached to housing (studios, laboratories, and individual offices), sometimes incorporated in little specialized centers: industrial or commercial units are each time reduced to the minimum viable size, destined for a minimum of persons. The same is true for hospitals and cultural establishments, the large number of which compensate for their dispersion and their generally reduced scale. All these cells (individual and social) are linked and **related** to each other by an abundant network of land and air routes: isolation has meaning only if it can be broken at any moment (Choay 1986:254).

The naturalist-culturalist model, which synthesized the urban and the rural, was conceived as the cure for the ills of unfettered nineteenth-century city growth. To the industrial functions of city buildings were added the signs of nature and of rural life. Daily living was returned to a human scale and mixed in with the routines of plant and animal life. Wright's "Broadacre" vision, in particular, has been quite influential despite having never been built. His proposed environment is not unlike today's suburban regions, if we discount the demand for four-acre homesites. He anticipated the emergence of shopping centers, regional malls, and suburban office or industrial parks. He also predicted the use of roadway underpasses and wide highways for auto traffic. As we shall discuss in Chapter 6, the nostalgic model that yearns for the small-town scale of the past remains an important inspiration for some contemporary planning, especially the new suburban environments of architects such as Duany and Krier (see Langdon 1994).

The Progressivist Planning Model

Unlike the nostalgic model, progressivist visions were oriented to the future and celebrated technological progress. At its core the ideology of progressivism depended on the concept of *modernity* and incorporated two distinct areas of development: first, the continual technological progress of industrial expansion, and, second, the innovations of avant-garde art such as cubism and abstract expressionism, which provided a departure from ordinary visual perspective. I shall discuss modernism more fully below, because, as a design movement, it was singularly responsible for the eradication of symbolic depth in contemporary cities until the recent period of thematic revival.

Ironically, while the progressivist model celebrated the symbols of technological advancement (such as the automobile) and the efficiency of progress, progressivist planning in practice avoided overt symbolic content and replaced the signifying city with an austere environment of concrete, steel, and glass in minimal geometric shapes such as the rectangular box of the high-rise office tower. Progressivism worked through iconic representation. As discussed in the previous chapter, icons are a type of sign but do not carry the symbolic baggage of intentional metaphorical associations. Modernist architects reduced all built forms to their iconic geometric shapes. This itself was a kind of theme, because the clean geometric forms came from the belief in progress through science and technology. Yet, the motif of progressivism was a creation of architects alone and their forms were cut off from the culture of the surrounding society. Furthermore, unlike architects of the previous Victorian period, progressive architects agreed with Adolf Loos that "ornament was a crime," and so they avoided overt symbols (Loos 1982).

The basis of progressivist city planning was the reduction of all urban spaces to their function, much as it had been done in the cities of early capitalism. Modernist architects took functionality to an extreme in order to promote efficiency. Thus, the credo of the times was "form follows function." Design was meant to stand in the service of efficient work and movement in the new environment. One leading architect of progressivism, Le Corbusier, conceived of the city as a "machine for living" or a tool that enabled continued progress and technological advancement. Conceived of as tools, all components of the city were reduced to their functions in order to make them work efficiently. Clean geometric forms became the norm for urban architecture. Thus, "progressivist planners carefully separate working zones from living zones, and living zones from civic centers or areas of recreation. Each of these categories is in turn divided into subcategories equally classified and ordered. Each type of work, administrative, industrial or commercial is assigned a label" (Choay 1986:247).

According to Le Corbusier, "Everything must be given form or set in order, in a condition of full efficiency" (1946:74). In his plan for the city of the future (the radiant city), transportation routes, for example, were based on automobile traffic and the superhighway. Le Corbusier's design abolished the street because it was the symbol of the chaotic, poorly planned industrial city. His radiant city reordered the space of the urban agglomeration. Instead of the haphazard placement of housing, which was usually low density, Le Corbusier planned large high-rise apartment blocks that liberated city space for use as parks and landscaped vistas. Equally important as functional efficiency was the desire of progressive architects, following the sentiments of Adolf Loos expressed above, to eradicate all sentimentality and traditional symbols within the city. Le Corbusier, for example, proposed a plan for the redevelopment of Paris that would eradicate all the picturesque old neighborhoods of the past. Nothing should get in the way of the modernist skyline and modernism's trace of abstract geometrical shapes as the urban landscape. In short,

> The planner "composes" his future city on the drawing board, as he would compose a painting. Following the principles of cubism, and still more those of purism and of Stijl, he eliminates every incidental detail in favor of simple forms, reduced to essentials, where the eye cannot stumble against any particularity; it is in a sense a question of constructing the a priori framework for any possible social behavior (Choay 1986:248).

The progressivist vision has had even more of an influence on city building than has the naturalist. Codified into the principles of modernist design and launched as a movement among architects around the globe, progressivism became known as the "international school" of architecture. Virtually every downtown center of every major city across the globe surrendered to the geometric rectangular boxes of high-rise buildings advocated by Le Corbusier. Superhighway construction demolished old neighborhoods and picturesque sections of the city in the obsessive promotion of "efficient" automobile traffic. In many places, planners obliterated low-density residential housing and replaced them with massive, high-rise buildings containing thousands of families in concentrated "projects." The outcome of decades of city building and renewal along progressivist lines, was, by the 1960s, a city space that was truly hyposignificant—lacking symbolic unity, austere and geometrical—with an absence of sentimentality and human-scaled social space along with its varied symbols of traditional cultures.

As a built environment, the modernist city celebrated the overarching theme of progress and technological efficiency. But, as a dream of the future, it contained enough internal contradictions to prevent its code from being carried forward into the next century. From the 1960s onward, the modernist city began to collapse under the weight of its own design failures as a human space.

Perhaps the best illustration of the limits encountered by the International School is the city of Brasilia in Brazil (Hoston, 1989). Built all at once as a unified project to house the federal government functions of the rapidly growing country, Brasilia was carved by modernist architects out of the undeveloped plateau country 600 miles from the inhabited coast. From the air the entire space resembles a bird and signifies the flight of Brazil toward a successful future. On the ground the bird motif was abandoned as the architects Lucio Costa and Oscar Niemeyer constructed an austere ode to Le Corbusier's principles of modernist design. The "death of the street" dictated that space would be dedicated to the automobile. Indeed, Brasilia has no streets, only superhighways that link gigantic, rectangular apartment blocks with each other. The huge buildings are separated by expansive but empty plazas meant as monuments rather than as usable spaces. The latter areas are ideal sites for the commission of crimes and, indeed, that is what has occurred. Because neighboring and local pedestrian interaction were eradicated by modernist design, the use of ramps, vacant parks, and concrete plazas by robbers and rapists has grown unchecked.

Inhabitants also complain that it is a very uncomfortable city in which to live. It lacks that human scale, warmth, and dynamism of street life that characterizes Brazilian cities elsewhere. Like the similarly inspired megahousing projects of the United States, such as the recently demolished Pruit-Igoe, Brasilia has failed as an urban space of habitation, while it breeds anonymity, alienation, and crime.

Consumption and the Modernist Transformation

As we have seen, early modernism accentuated the decline of symbolic elements in the built environment that began in the nineteenth century with the emergence of the capitalist-industrial city. Functions rather than symbolic allusions came to dominate urban decor, while the richness of signification was confined to the homes of the wealthy and to inner city religious practices. During the early twentieth century this trend of hyposignification intensified through the deployment of modernist design practices. Our discussion of social shifts so far has focused on the process of building and the production of material culture. In contrast, the process of consumption of commodities and the use of the built environment, which is the domain of the urban masses, involves its own dynamic of thematic interplay. In particular, while architects and planners were busy distancing themselves from traditional material forms endowed with signification, the selling of commodities and the creation of consumer spaces could not quite do without symbols and meaningful themes.

For much of the nineteenth century vestigial symbolism was woven into the urban fabric of what was otherwise the chaotic melange of the industrial city. For the most part the emergent bourgeoisie played a one-note theme of urban culture that reinforced its high status and celebrated the acquisition of wealth. In the early 1800s members of the bourgeoisie borrowed most of the symbols from the grand stages of empires and royalty. Particularly in the home, decor favored by the middle classes deployed an eclectic mix of Elizabethan, Egyptian, or Italian rococo motifs that signified wealth, privilege, and luxury (Rybczynski 1986). As Veblen (1899) so acutely observed almost 100 years ago, the consumption patterns of the successful American business elite emphasized luxury, ostentation, and "conspicuous consumption," which were all signs of opulence and success in contrast to the drab, debilitating, and poverty-stricken lives of the great mass of urban and rural workers. Interior design of the times developed an eclectic look, known as the "Queen Anne" style, by borrowing heavily from the opulent and aristocratic signs of English nobility.

In contrast, the traditional homes, like the ones lived in by the working and lower-middle classes, were dominated by patriarchy and endowed with cultural signs of family life. Until the 1920s the only real rival to the richness of this kind of signification was the desire of the working and middle classes to ape the aristocracy and its opulent home furnishings. Therefore, home interiors at the time either copied the style of the upper class or displayed the haphazard decor of family-centered working class life. Just as architecture and the productionist ideologies of twentieth century capitalism were changed forever by the International School and its design philosophy of modernism, so, too, was the interior of the home transformed by the juggernaut of modernist designers. After 1920, and under the spell of modernism, housing interiors were commodified and, therefore, changed forever.

Modernist Interior Design

The changes made in the traditional home by modernist design are the subject of Jean Baudrillard's study, *The System of Objects* (1968). He highlights the important role played by the module. Each room of the home, which was formerly the repository of objects that symbolized either past or present family life and were, therefore, endowed with strong affect and meaning, became a target in the 1920s and 1930s for commodification according to modernist design. The concept of the "ensemble," which was already a powerful normative standard in women's fashion, was extended to home furnishings through the modular mechanism of the "set." Designers sold "kitchen sets" for the kitchen, "living room sets" for the living room, and "bathroom sets" for the bathroom. What counted most in this new logic of home decoration was not the symbolic value of the individual objects themselves, as happened in the traditional home, but how well each particular object belonging to a "set" fit in with every other object of the set. The symbolic value of interior furnishings, in short, passed from the valorized emotional meanings of family life, including signs of past family and their experience, to the limited meaning of being "fashionable" or "up-to-date," that is, of being "modern." This change cut off people living in modernist-designed homes from the emotion laden signs of family and personal history.

The milieu of modernity changed the value of common household objects from affective symbols of family background to functional tools of living, as Le Corbusier suggested. Baudrillard (1968:26) argues that this is clearly illustrated by the example of the clock. Most commonly the large "grandfather" clock displayed in the traditional home was not only an imposing time piece but also a family memento often inherited over several generations. Modernist design practice replaced this heirloom with an abstract object that simply denoted the time and could be hung anywhere. The symbolic value of the modernist clock is only that it is "modern," that is, fashionable, so that its owners identify themselves with being up to date. For example, in 1930, the Cincinnati Victor Company, manufacturer of electric clocks, advertised their "Waverly" model for the kitchen. "Finished in a beautiful chromium plate, it harmonizes with the *modern* [emphasis added] mode in kitchen decoration. The Waverly is also offered in several attractive colors to match any particular color scheme" (Pages of Time, 1951).

With the transition from family heirloom to a simple timepiece, the clock as home object is divested of its affective, symbolic value as a signifier of intergenerational continuity and becomes a functional tool. As Francoise Choay argues, modernist design reduced the symbolic content of the environment to the signification of function alone, and it became, therefore, hyposignificant or attenuated in meaning. As Jean Baudrillard notes, traditional symbolism in the home was eradicated by the domination of commodified furnishings through modernist design practice. This divestiture of the symbolic content of daily life through abstract design and consumerism set the stage for the vengeful return of meaning and symbolism that we are currently experiencing, which I call "the themed environment."

Consumer Shopping Spaces and Symbolic Themes

Despite the assault by modernist symbols in the built environment, places remained in the great industrial cities of Europe and the United States where the limited deployment of themes prevailed. The signifiers of wealth and status structured the marketing of housing. Interiors proclaimed the new and the fashionable in home furnishings. Denotation of function is a minimalist mode of signification, yet it retained a certain symbolic value through an association with modernist design, that is, the connotation of progress or being "up-to-date." The home, however, was only one venue of consumerism in the early twentieth century. As the middle class grew in both numbers and affluence it became the target for new marketing schemes that sought to increase the sheer volume of consumer purchasing through the delivery of a wide array of commodities.

The culmination of the new marketing impulse that predated modernism in Europe was the invention in nineteenth-century Paris of the "department store" (see Williams, 1982; Miller, 1981; Leach, 1993). The first such store, which opened in 1869, was the Bon Marché. Every commodity was identified by function and grouped with every other associated commodity into "departments." This structure liberated consumers from the confines of appearing before the retail clerk, and they could move around freely, coming into direct contact with merchandise. Fantasies and themes of consumerism remained limited at this time and were restricted to the usual ones of exoticism (such as the sale of imported commodities like silk) and opulence (for perfumes, home furnishings, fashions, and the like) within the new marketing structure. Because Paris was the fashion capital of the world, and because the department store was so successful as a generator of profit, entrepreneurs such as Marshall Field in Chicago and Gimbals Brothers in New York copied the department store form in the late 1800s and used its themes to sell goods in the United States.

The success of large department stores changed the structure of labor in the cities by moving it away from dependency on manufacturing alone. Certain service occupations emerged that were closely connected to the promotion of consumer purchasing and the display of commodities within department stores. Window dressers, for example, developed their art of adorning mannequins in store displays for the benefit of the passerby. Stores used theatrical techniques of staging, lighting, and posing to great effect. Employment in the sales-related occupations exploded. In addition, advertising and pictorial promotional displays began to play an increasing role in the stimulation of consumer desire and in the promotion of particular commodities. These images affected our culture.

The advertising industry developed in tandem with the great department stores, including the phenomenal mail order business initiated by Sears, Roebuck and Company and its catalogue that potentially could be sent to every home in America. As elsewhere within the decor of department stores, pictorial advertising exploited the same limited themes of luxury and exoticism. Many consumer outlets now included the exoticism of technological progress as exemplified in the so-called mechanical marvels of household "laborsaving" devices. These commodities signified the theme of progress that was the basis of the modernist code.

The Persistence of Themed Environments

Although the premise of the above discussion is that the modernist period, unlike previous design codes, discouraged the use of symbols and themes in the built environment, it would be quite wrong to suggest that everyday milieus did not exploit symbolic motifs even in the 1920s and 1930s. We have already seen that, despite its limited scope, department stores and home furnishings aggressively promoted fantasies of wealth, exoticism and technological progress. Other symbolic and emotive environments, such as the department store form, also appeared during the late nineteenth century and influence consumer spaces to this day. Some of these additional themed environments were the state fairs,

A large urban department store that caters to the pedestrian crowds of the city. Photo courtesy of UPI/Bettmann.

world expositions, arcades, and amusement zones of the turn of the century industrial societies. In addition, a new source of symbols emerged in the increasing development of suburban communities during this period.

World Expositions

World expositions, such as the previously mentioned Columbian Exposition of 1893 in Chicago, were attempts by society to reaffirm its belief in progress as its large cities sunk further into the mire of social problems associated with unbridled capitalist industrialization. The expositions of the nineteenth century were utopian dreams staged against the real nightmare of uneven development found in cities, that is, the contrast between the great success of urban capitalism, on the one hand, and its immense social problems such as homelessness, poverty, and frequent health crises, on the other. International world's fairs, which began in the late nineteenth century in Europe, were combination trade fairs for the benefit of major commodity producers and the reassuring celebration of the planner's or architect's vision for the improved urban milieu of tomorrow. They contained elaborate representations of utopian schemes for an enriched everyday life. Expositions promoted middle class consumption as the social norm. They presented the plethora of commodities made available by the economic system in a whimsical and amusing way. Consumption itself was promoted as a form of amusement. In the best modernist style, the world expositions reinforced the social belief in the benefits of technological advancement and in the ability of people to plan for a promised age of capitalist cornucopia.

According to David Frisby, "The world expositions were the high school in which the masses, dragged away from consumption, learned to empathize with exchange value: 'Look at everything, touch nothing.' Their goal as far as the masses were concerned was distraction" (1985:254).

The greatest fair of the nineteenth century was the Columbian Exposition, which opened May 1, 1893, in Chicago on 6,000 acres of land by Lake Michigan and the University of Chicago. Over four hundred thousand people visited this event, including President Grover Cleveland. Among its most popular attractions was the transportation building designed by Louis Sullivan in a new style of urban construction that contained a projected utopian scheme for the plan of future cities. Years later, at the New York World's Fair in 1938, the utopian representation of tomorrow contained in the transportation building was again the popular hit of the exposition. Then the automobile had been introduced as a mass-marketed product and fantasizing about progress had shifted from dreams of an extensive railroad web of public transportation to a futuristic model of efficient auto highway networks and self-propelled cars. People's belief in modernism meant that all the problems of getting to and from work could be solved through the purchase of a single commodity—the family car.

World Fairs such as the 1970s fair in Seattle, which is responsible for the famous space needle, continue to alter our urban landscapes. They are uniquely modernist in idea, because they unabashedly celebrate the notion of progress and the benefits to people of continued technological innovation. Therefore, they can be contrasted with the "postmodern" designs of today, that is, the increasing skepticism about technological advancement and the growing recognition that progress is a mixed blessing. As a form of space, however, world fairs are excellent examples of themed environments because they incorporate sign systems as a way of communicating to onlookers the signification of buildings and exhibits, both regarding what the displays stand for as symbols and what they seek to compel visitors to do or how to behave in the exposition spaces. In a postmodern world these fairs might have limited value as purveyors of utopian visions, but they nevertheless remain useful as occasions for corporations to explore alternate themed environments that might improve the marketing of their products.

There is another aspect of the world fair expositions of the nineteenth century that directly bears the seeds of postmodernism. These gigantic pedestrian-oriented carnivals of industrialism were the precursors of today's theme parks, such as Disneyland. As market fairs that enlarged and developed fantasy themes, as pedestrian and open-air environments, and as diversions offering entertaining rides and attractions, they worked out the important articulation between fantasy marketing schemes projecting the future as conceived by giant corporations and a built environment that was diversionary and fun. It is but a small step, in other words, from the World's Fair of 1938 in Flushing Meadows, New York City, which entertained millions of visitors during the depression and the approach of World War II, to Disneyland, which was erected in 1955 in suburban Anaheim in southern California.

Urban Arcades

Another nineteenth century adaption to commodity capitalism was the urban arcade that is the forerunner of the fully enclosed shopping mall of the present. The social critic Walter Benjamin (1969) considered the arcade as the preeminent modernist form. By arcade I mean the often labrynthian, enclosed city pathways that were pedestrian thoroughfares lined with small shops of all kinds. Within the arcade, or, with a walk through an arcade, the pedestrian becomes a consumer and, as Benjamin notes, is stimulated to dream of life in a "primeval landscape of consumption" and abundance. The arcade shops, with their varied kinds of merchandise, embody the increasing variety of commodity fantasies, or "phantasmagoria," that were beginning to appear in the 1920s because of the rising purchasing power and sheer numbers of the growing middle class. The consumer arcade, through the mediation of its shops, introduced the new and stylish to the urban masses. This made it the purveyor of the modernist experience—that is, the experience of the new, of the unique, of the stimulation of desire for novel material objects, or, as Benjamin said, of "wish symbols."

The arcades of Paris, which Benjamin studied in the 1920s, were a permanent world's exposition. They were not only the staging areas for consumer fantasies or the promoters of new fantasies but also the primal ground for the development of a new kind of subjectivity—one based on "being a consumer," on the stimulation of a desiring, commodity-craving self. It was a qualitative departure from the nineteenth century self socialized by the routine work-a-day world of industrial factories and their everyday life. Arcade shops functioned together as a permanent exposition or fair. They did not rely on creating new consumer fantasies but on amplifying and developing already existing themes of desire. Either they glorified opulence, luxury, and symbols of wealth, or they introduced the exotic, the new, the import, and the technological or mechanical marvel that you were invited to believe you could not live without. This development of commodity fantasy themes by the arcade shops fed the growing activity of the advertising industry that circulated the new, amplified images from the central city arcades to the surrounding social spaces across the nation.

In this manner, the early arcades provided a key channel of desire to a society increasingly reliant on themed environments. They were the material link between the growing power of the advertising industry with its promotion of consumer fantasies and the varied products of the economy that shifted progressively toward commodity production and, lately, toward pure images, rather than heavy manufacturing.

Suburbia

In Chapter 1 I discussed how suburbanization at the turn of the century by the wealthy introduced certain themes to visions of daily life. The motifs of affluence, excess, and conspicuous consumption were also deployed through estate living outside the large, industrial city. As suburban development increased in popularity for the middle class in the years of the early twentieth century, the same themes celebrating wealth and prestige dominated housing and landscaping choices. By the 1920s there was enough demand for suburban homes that developers could switch from custom building to the construction of a modest number of mass-produced houses within a single new community. Early suburban developments that appeared then, such as Tuxedo Park outside of New York City, Lake Forest near Chicago, and Shaker Heights eight miles from downtown Cleveland, stressed the symbolic significance of their locations by extolling their exclusivity, prestige, and affluence.

A nineteenth century urban arcade—the precursor of the mall. These arcades were usually composed of small shops that were called boutiques. Recently the downtown section of Las Vegas was remodeled into a covered, arcade form (see Chapter 5). Photo courtesy of Corbis-Bettmann.

Developers and real estate agents responsible for attracting home buyers to these areas advertised their ethnic and racial exclusion while celebrating these locations as symbols of status and wealth. In this early period of suburban development, Catholics, Jews, and blacks were excluded from purchasing homes by racist developers and real estate agents. It was not, however, until after World War II that suburban residence became available to the masses of Americans, although blacks remained excluded from most suburban housing. Today the majority of people in the United States live in the suburban areas of our large, metropolitan regions.

Single-family homes in sprawling developments outside the large city borrow several symbolic features from the original "nouveaux riches" mansions. They ape signs of social prestige and individual affluence. Their front lawns are scaled down mini-versions of those found on estates but are also made symbols of excess. Left idle to grow grass, the lawns of typical middle class homes require constant work, usually from the man of the house or a contracted lawn service. In contrast, the wealthy owners of nineteenth-century country mansions kept gardeners on their staffs. Suburban backyards also retain the estate function of recreation and leisure. Front doors and driveways are marked off to signify prestige. Even mailboxes are stylized for the same reason. As in the large country estates, middle class suburban homes come equipped with a separate kitchen and dining room. Owners also reserve the latter for special occasions.

Although all these similarities with the conspicuous consumption of the wealthy serve as signs of status, they are also scaled down replicas that fit the more modest budget of middle-class home owners. In this sense, normative plans for suburban housing, the kind of floor layout that people expect when purchasing such homes, use iconic representation to recall directly the referent code of nineteenth-century estate life. Consequently, the material elements of today's suburban housing are both signs of status and iconic representations drawing on our familiarity with the cultural code of the upper class American (and English) estate. Without the cultural conditioning of the latter, we might find the land use of suburban housing and the features dedicated as signs of excess quite odd.

Once a mass market for suburban housing was created, after World War II, the population shift to these areas outside the large city accelerated. Government programs, such as the mortgage interest tax deduction, made it profitable to own a house rather than rent. People were attracted to the suburbs because of the prestige. As competition heated up among many developers, however, status appeals were not enough to differentiate one company's housing from another. Consequently, builders resorted to differentiating their essentially similar products through symbols. They used exotic and fantasy themes for development names. The mundane "Levittown" of the 1940s gave way to the less ordinary "Mountain Estates" or the exotic "Wildwood Homes." Streets and home models themselves were also endowed with thematically stylized names, such as "River Run," "Bird Wing," and "Maui Court." All this symbolic work stood alongside terrains that showed little evidence of mountains, nature, or tropical scenery. Yet, symbolic naming and the search for labels with ever increasing appeal currently characterizes our environment.

In short, although the earliest symbolic themes of wealth, prestige, and exclusion were played out repeatedly as one-note symphonies in the development of large industrial cities, these motifs were embellished over the years in residential locations outside the metropolitan areas. After 1940, more people were allowed to participate in this great spectacle of success due to the explosion of affluence occurring after World War II. A kind of status or prestige was marketed to the masses symbolized by the affordability of the single-family suburban home. Ancillary themes signifying wealth through iconic signs of excess or conspicuous consumption were also developed even by the most modest suburban developments, such as the original Levittown. Finally, suburbanization and mass construction introduced the phenomenon of business competition using symbols that is so characteristic of the consumer society now. Through the use of these signs, suburbanization, like the arcades and expositions of the time, maintained a certain level of signification, while the larger environment of the industrial city made little use of connotative symbols.

As discussed in Chapter 1, the large industrial city of the nineteenth and early twentieth century could hardly be called a themed environment. Cities then were hyposignificant, that is, their symbolic content was attenuated and limited to signifying functionality—the bank was a sign of banking, the factory a sign of manufacturing, and the working class home a sign of shelter or neighborhood. Yet, despite this limited use of symbols, world fairs, the phantasmagoria of commercial arcades, and the proliferation of suburban residential development introduced certain symbolic motifs that laid the groundwork for a shift to a themed environment. The efforts prior to the 1950s were quite modest and consisted almost entirely in the celebration of affluence, conspicuous consumption, and prestige.

As time went on the modernist stranglehold on building and planning declined. After 1950 architects and planners reacted against hyposignification. Symbols returned to the milieu of daily life. Now there is an increasing reliance on themes in all aspects of our culture. Furthermore, spaces have become more entertaining. Our present culture is composed of a confluence of media entertainment and the built environment. Before analyzing these milieus, such as restaurants, malls, and theme parks, I shall explain in the next chapter why the trend to themes has occurred and how it is connected to the needs of a consumer-oriented, profit-making society that is currently dominated by a media culture (Postman, 1985; Kellner, 1995).

The Mirror
of Production:
The Realization
Problem of Capital

In the previous chapter I used the example of the increasing competition among suburban developers of housing to show the strong connection between economic needs and the reliance on motifs in the marketing of commodities. This link is very important in understanding both the function and the increasing use of themed environments in our society. What is true for the sale of housing also holds for other commodities. Increasingly, suppliers of all types of consumer products compete with each other through symbolic differences. During the period of early capitalist industrialism, in the eighteenth and nineteenth centuries, economic competition meant competition through production—the need simultaneously to reduce costs and to manufacture products in quantity. Today these production criteria remain important but there is a second aspect—thematic competition or competition through variation in symbols among products in any particular market.

Clearly, the affordability of commodities rules the act of consumption, but presently the use of thematic appeals in marketing also regulates the social process of consuming. In the past, people acted as consumers by relating the prices of things to their respective budgets. Common, rational calculation ruled consumer behavior. Now, to this monetary relation, has been added a second dimension. The consumption process also consists of a link between fantasies of self-fulfillment through commodities and ordinary consumer needs. Many of these symbolic motifs that exploit basic desires appeal to people despite their inability to afford commodities associated with them. Thus, to the relation of consumers to prices and budgets, which has always underlain individual behavior in a capitalist system, the consumption process has added the relation between customers and commodities with expressed symbolic images. Furthermore, the importance of the *symbolic* value of commodities, engineered by mass marketing, advertising, and TV commercials, among other sources, has grown considerably over the years. Presently, the price-consumption link, which once dominated consumer choices, is now joined by the symbolic value-consumption link, which involves considerations of a personal, sign-oriented nature in the purchase of consumer goods.

Due to the importance of motifs in marketing, the current economy is quite different from that of 100 years ago. The present global relation between economic processes and the use of themes reflects significant historical changes because of fundamental shifts in the organization of capitalism itself. This chapter explains the current dependency of both production and consumption on symbolic appeals, besides considerations of production costs, profits, prices, and budgets.

The Mirror of Production

Modern economic analysis stresses the world of production. This was most explicit for Karl Marx who dissected the capitalist system and exposed the conflict at its core between workers and owners of factories. In all approaches to the understanding of capitalism, however, the same basic relation applies. Capitalists invest money, or "capital," in a productive enterprise, usually involving manufacturing and the employment of an industrial work force, which then produces a "commodity." They then sell this product in a "market." When the costs of production and marketing are subtracted from this "market price," the remainder is "profit," or more capital. The owner of the factory, or "capitalist," can then take this capital, reinvest it in the factory and expand production, or invest it somewhere else in another capital market. Pure profit is pure money under capitalism and can flow to any source of investment that has the potential to make even more money. Marx summarized this dynamic by his famous formula: $M \rightarrow C \rightarrow M'$, that is, money, or M, is invested in commodity production, C, which, when sold, becomes more money, or M'.

This scheme seems simple and in many ways it is. Just about anyone with some money can set up a business and become a capitalist. Many people attempt just that, but few succeed. Contingencies arising in the "real world" of making money are quite unforgiving in a capitalist-competitive system. Among all the complications that arise when applying the $M \rightarrow C \rightarrow M'$ schema to reality, the most formidable one is contained within that formula, but has been neglected for years by analysts, including Marx himself. Early analysts of capitalism focused on the first step in the equation, namely, the conversion of money to commodity production within the environment of the factory. Studies of the rise of capitalism as a social system concentrate on the emergence of the social conditions that have produced the supply of industrial workers, on the one hand, and a class of capitalists freed from the authority of church and landed traditions, on the other. This social organization forms the basis for the accumulation of capital through commodity production.

For many years the second step in the formula, or the conversion from commodities, "C," to more money, or "M′," was simply assumed. Today, we know that this last step is quite problematical. People in business, even those with immense inventories and productive potential, have considerable difficulty unloading their products on the market in a successful manner that enables them to enjoy reasonable profits. Consider the domestic automobile industry in the United States. In the 1950s the production of cars employed one of every six workers in some capacity. The U.S. automobile industry also supported the U.S. steel industry, its tire industry, its battery, brake and shock absorber industries, and so on. By the 1970s, due to foreign competition, people were simply not buying American cars in the immense volumes of the past. Demand remained high, but alternate, competitive commodities were available as imports. The step from M, money, to C, commodities, remained in high gear for a time for domestic automobile manufacturers, but they found it increasingly more difficult to move from the large inventories of commodities, or C, to their sale and subsequent reconversion into profit, or M′.

In fact, the drop in the volume of sales produced a critical and long-lasting crisis in American capitalism. As sales declined and companies readjusted to a more competitive global environment, they reduced their own labor forces and canceled orders of steel, batteries, and tires, throwing those industries also into decline. These critical adjustments, which are called "deindustrialization" (Piore and Sabel 1984; Harvey 1988) brought entire industries that formerly were tied to the production of cars to their knees. By the 1990s, the United States was no longer the largest manufacturer of steel or cars and its domestic companies had to function in an operating environment where the conversion from commodity in the market to profit is increasingly less certain.

The above example and its shifting dynamics of the capitalist accumulation process from an emphasis on manufacturing to a focus on the dynamics of profit-making in a globally competitive environment illustrates a previously neglected problem area of capitalism known as the "realization" of capital. It is the transfer of value from the commodity to its realization in sales, rather than the manufacturing process, which has become increasingly riddled with both risks and voracious competition for contemporary capitalists. The production, or manufacturing, process simply "valorizes" commodities by creating value in production. In order for capitalists to "realize" that extra value, they must sell the goods they produce. Only after the sale can companies count up their profit and only *if* they are successful in making a profit on sales can capitalists remain alive for the next cycle of accumulation. The conversion from C to M´ is increasingly more critical to the dynamics of capitalist accumulation as the world becomes a more competitive place. This frames the "realization problem" of our society and its aggregate solution has led us to a themed environment.

The Realization of Capital

When Karl Marx and other nineteenth-century analysts of capitalism wrote about economic development they neglected the realization problem, although they mentioned and were aware of it. More important for them, as we have discussed, was the dynamics of production, the problems with an industrial labor force, and the complexities of profit-making in a world of competitive capitalists and landlords. In the twentieth century it has become more important for the survival of capitalism to succeed in the realization and circulation of capital through commodity production within an environment that remains highly competitive. The issue for the continued expansion of capital is no longer so much the problem of production, or capital valorization in commodities at the factory, but of consumption, or capital realization at the market.

Baudrillard and the Political Economy of the Sign

More than any other contemporary observer of society, the French postmodernist, Jean Baudrillard, has called attention to the new conditions under which capitalism is now developing and from which its future survival depends. For Baudrillard, the realization problem of capital, rather than the valorization problem of factory-based industrialization, currently stands at the very core of capitalism's historical dynamics.

Baudrillard unveiled his thesis in a series of books that began with a frontal attack on Karl Marx. In 1975 he published *The Mirror of Production*, which was a critique of Marx's *Capital*. According to Baudrillard, Karl Marx was misguided. He failed to understand the true dynamic of capitalism that was less about the world of the factory and the conversion of an agricultural labor force to the regime of industrial production than about the world of the market and the conversion of laborers of all kinds to consumers. Without the latter change in the society of modernity and postmodernity, products of manufacture would simply rot in the marketplace while the emergent capitalist class would return to a world of abjection and immiseration. Capitalism succeeded because it produced goods that the masses of workers could afford and purchased. The realization of capital, in Baudrillard's view, was the precondition for the growth of the productive powers of the capitalist system, whereas Marx emphasized the historical dynamic of the production process itself.

Baudrillard (1973) considers political economy and especially the Marxian approach as lost in the spell of the "mirror of production." It sees things in reflection by emphasizing production as the central process of capitalist accumulation. Instead, it is the act of consumption that is at the base of the survival of capitalism and this act depends more on the transformation of individuals into desiring free-spending consumers than into industrial workers. All of the concerns that Marx and other political economists possessed regarding the role of the workers in the historical development of capitalism were misguided. Instead, the critical dynamics of capitalist development hinges on the ability to *realize* capital once commodities are produced.

Baudrillard claims that the record has borne him out. The industrial countries of the West have not developed into revolutionary, anticapitalist societies but into voracious consumer nations focused on the desire for commodities. Furthermore, as is well documented by studies lamenting deindustrialization (see Bluestone and Harrison 1982), manufacturing and the world of factories have declined in the American landscape. Production is increasingly being moved offshore to newly developing countries. Thus, there is still an entire capitalist universe of production where the dynamics of conversion from capital, or M, to commodities, or C, reigns supreme. But as the working force of the United States can attest, that process occurs progressively more in areas outside the country. The population of this society remains burdened with the task of completing the "realization" side of the capital accumulation equation. Its way of working has changed, most commonly by shifting to information and/or service industries, but their role as happy consumers of capital's bounty remains, even if the goods that make up that cornucopia are increasingly imported.

Baudrillard maintains that the mirror image of capitalism fooled Marx and other political economists into focusing on manufacturing and the creation of an industrial work force during the 19th century. Instead the important dynamics of development in the 20th century, especially since the Great Depression of the 1930s, concern consumption, competition among capitalists in the global market, and the behavior of people as consumers rather than workers. Nowhere is this more accurate than in the United States—a net importer of goods, with a trade deficit in the billions of dollars. Other nations, such as Japan and Singapore, have become "export-led economies" whose very existence depends on the level of imports by nations like the United States. While political economy of the nineteenth century variety, like that of Marx, might pertain to those export-led economies, it is consumption dynamics, not production, that is most relevant to the continual well being of the United States.

The Role of Symbols
or Themes in the Circuit of Capital

A nation of consumers must be fed by appeals to consume even when the goods they are offered have dubious use-values. Basic human needs are relatively simple and consist, as every third grade school child can attest, mainly of food, clothing, and shelter—not to mention a job that can provide for these necessities. The needs pumping up a consumer society, however, extend much beyond these basics, and, even the basics are elaborated by the practice of consumption almost beyond recognition from the picture painted for school children. Shelter, for most people, for example, means a basic three or four bedroom suburban house complete with a fully-equipped kitchen and recreation room. Consumers also view the commodities that stock such a "basic" home as "necessities." They desire dishwashers, refrigerators, microwave ovens, conventional ovens, stoves, and assorted electric gadgets in the kitchen. In other rooms they want television sets, video tape players, stereo equipment, compact disk players, portable phones, leisure furniture and bedroom sets. Almost all these commodities are either manufactured entirely abroad or contain many components manufactured abroad. Our principal task in this country, as we have shifted away from industrial production, has become that of desiring these goods as necessities with which we cannot do without in our daily life.

For the most part, the production of desire for such commodities at the intense level that exists in our society depends directly on symbolic mechanisms—on a commercial culture. Signs and themes play a central role in the proper priming of the consumer society. We may agree with Baudrillard that symbolic processses solve the realization problem of capital. This process will be illustrated below, but before doing so, it is also necessary to demonstrate how central are symbolic processes to the entire circuit of capital. The role of meaning systems, once referred to almost exclusively by the overused concept of "ideology," has been essential to capitalist development since its earliest beginnings in the competitive cauldrons of European merchant towns. The history of capital is a history of the role of signification and meaning systems in the economic life of society. This role is not confined merely to the marketing of commodities. Rather, the entire process of capital accumulation is shot through with mechanisms that depend on symbolic processes for their proper functioning.

Signs and the Constitution of a "Capitalist Class"

Karl Marx's Class Emphasis

Karl Marx's analysis of capitalist development in his classic work, *Capital* (1868), provides us with an understanding of the political economy of its history. Marx is concerned to show, in this work, not only how the capitalist system operates but how it began and grew naturally as a consequence of the economic forces that it unleashed in the world. The agent of growth was the capitalist class, a collection of individuals who often competed ruthlessly with one another, but who nevertheless were like-minded in the way they operated. Their interests and style of activity were relatively new to organized society until the eighteenth and nineteenth centuries, although business people in many other countries during countless other times acted in ways that might be considered similar. The capitalist class of Marx's analysis fixated on the extraction of the greatest level of production and profit from the workers it had at its disposal. The purpose of economic activity was to *accumulate* money that would be invested and reinvested repeatedly in business to acquire more wealth. The drive to accumulate was not mollified by any social or family considerations that formerly constrained typical business people, such as religious proscriptions against usury (the lending of money at rates of interest), the social squeamishness that might accompany the employment of child laborers, the heartless demand for long days of work, or payment in wages rather than in kind—leaving the laborers to fend for themselves in commodity markets to supply the sustenance of life.

Early capitalists were also hardened by their own fate should they fail in business and wind up in debtors prison or in the employ of previous competitors. They felt no moral or social obligation to provide for the welfare of their workers. If the wage they paid was not sufficient to care for the family needs of laborers, they did not consider the matter their concern unless it forced the workers to organize and demand higher wages. In that case, they invested part of their expanding monetary resources in the hiring of guards, goons, or politicians to force adversarially inclined employees to comply with the capitalist class's conditions of work. In short, the capitalist class of Marx's analysis was immune to the social, religious, and moral failings of their efforts as long as these did not interfere with their fundamental goal of the maximum extraction of wealth from the production process and its accumulation as capital over time.

Individuals during the European middle ages were no strangers to the suffering of common people in everyday life. However, they did not live in a social world of values or norms that supported what later became the obvious excesses of early capitalism—especially the growth of poverty in the cities. Marx's analysis does not answer the question of how fundamental values could change to accommodate the new logic of capital. His work remains primarily focused on the economic and political shifts that resulted in the structural development, in western Europe, of a capitalist society, that is, a society ruled by capitalist principles. The cultural adjustments that had to occur so that the new order could not only come into being but also reproduce itself were neglected in Marx's analysis. According to Marx and subsequent Marxists, reproduction of the new order occurred because capitalism created a world of *necessity* that compelled individuals, both workers and capitalists, to behave in the appropriate manner. But, for many other students of society, this answer begs the question of how the social norms of accumulation dominated society. Room remained open to appreciate the role of cultural factors in a way not practiced by Marxists who tended to emphasize only economic and political concerns in historical development. An important qualification and partial critique of Karl Marx's work on capitalism, therefore, was needed to illuminate the cultural factors at work in capitalism. Max Weber (1968), a founding father of academic sociology at the turn of the century, provided a solution to some, if not all, of these issues.

Max Weber and Modes of Consciousness
Weber, like Marx, was interested in explaining broad historical movements and change. Unlike Marx, however, he merely treated economic factors as one among several that served to develop society. He did not disagree with Marx nor with Marx's understanding of capitalism, for example, but he did seek to highlight factors in its development that were downplayed by Marx's analysis. Concerning broad sweeps of history, Weber was particularly inclined to emphasize the way modes of consciousness helped to organize productive forces. In this concern, he was not unique. Marx before Weber, like all good German historicists, also focused on the role ideas and values played in causing social change. Marx's interest was in what he called ideology, which was a set of beliefs that prevailed within a particular historical epoch and served to provide a framework of understanding for social collectivities, particularly classes, in interpreting the events of daily life. In this sense, Marx's concept of ideology was essentially *political*. Conceptual universes that were used to "explain" the meaning of everyday life were, for Marx, frameworks that enabled social groups, and, in particular, classes such as capitalists, workers, and landlords, to articulate political positions compared to the struggle over dividing resources and wealth in any given social system.

Weber was also concerned with the role states of consciousness played in daily life, but unlike Marx, he was interested in the way individual ideas meld with group understandings. Thus, Weber, more than Marx, was focused on individuals and more abstract in his treatment of states of consciousness because he treated those states as autonomous and as powerful causal factors of action in their own right. When viewing the grand sweep of history, Marx focused on the struggle over wealth. When Weber looked at the same sweep, he was more intrigued by the way modes of thinking organized action into social forces and systems. Marx studied how a capitalist money economy forced individuals to become increasingly rational in their handling of productive resources and investment dollars. Otherwise, they would be beaten in competition with other more rational capitalists.

Weber studied how rational thinking was increasingly apparent as an autonomous force in the organization of *every* aspect of modern societies, irrespective of the particular capitalist (that is economic) context. Weber considered "instrumental rationality" as the most potent social force in the development of modern society. By this concept he meant *goal-directed thinking* divorced from tradition, religion, or emotion, which was efficient and abstractly organized by rules. According to Weber, the historical development of society progressed from periods dominated by religious beliefs, traditions, and particular customs to the contemporary period where social organization uses strict rational calculations of means to ends, abstract thinking that eschews emotions and religious beliefs, and the *efficient* deployment of rule-directed behavior.

Weber went over the same historical ground as Marx and attempted an explanation for the rise and subsequent success of the capitalist social system in the West. He agreed with Marx regarding the economic and political forces that caused success. However, he went much further than Marx in describing the way modes of consciousness were powerful causal factors during capitalism's development. More specifically, he showed how certain social groups produced by cultural changes were possessed with legitimated logics of action that were well suited to the dominance of capitalist relations in society and may have helped bring it about.

The groups most intriguing to Weber were the early Protestant sects of medieval Europe that stressed individual fate or states of grace which sanctioned the single minded pursuit of profit, or accumulation, as a goal of action. For these sects, according to Weber, success in the accumulation of capital was a sign of god's favoritism. They adopted instrumentally rational methods of business, divorced from emotional or traditional social considerations, in the pursuit of the goal of capital accumulation and investment. Weber, in a famous book, *The Protestant Ethic and the Spirit of Capitalism*, explained how critical this spirit of instrumental rationality applied to the accumulation of capital was for the eventual domination of the capitalist class in European society. By so doing he also demonstrated that symbolic meaning remained a potent social force in the functioning of society—even for the advanced capitalist society that had abandoned tradition and group sentiments that placed individuals above monetary concerns—because instrumental reason was sacred to the Protestant belief system.

In Weber's view the most rational, functional, and calculating consciousness was still embedded in a larger cultural complex of symbols, or a universe of meaning, which functioned to both construct and explain the meaning of daily life. Religious belief and the strictly rational calculation of business could still develop hand in hand. In addition, cultural symbols were as autonomous in the explanation of historical change as were the material factors of economic development and political struggle so important to Karl

Marx. For Weber, this was so precisely because cultural symbols held power as expressions of modes of action. They directed action toward specific goals. They were, in short, the engines of will and behavior. With capitalism, the affinity between certain Protestant sects and the single-minded desire to accumulate capital despite its human consequences, became the driving force behind its early success in Europe. In fact, Weber showed how success in business was *interpreted* as a sign of grace, while failure in business was a sign of spiritual disfavor. Early Protestant sects possessed a mode of thinking that liberated the individual from the social responsibility for the negative outcomes of capital accumulation, such as poverty, homelessness, child abandonment, and the failure of business within the commercial class, although they were encouraged to respond to these ills as individuals. Socially negative consequences of capitalism were symbols of a lack of grace, that is, they could be explained religiously without the need to defend either success or failure as a social concern.

In short, for both Marx and Weber, the cutthroat world of early capitalism possessed systems of meaning that worked to explain daily life for its inhabitants, despite the domination of functional economic and monetary needs. Marx focused on the sets of beliefs, or ideologies, which groups used to either understand or justify their social positions as economic agents; whereas Weber acknowledged these ideologies but also showed how independent religious (cultural) ideas specifically fit the conditions of early capitalism so that the groups propagating them were also the source of capitalist expansion and development. Both Marx and Weber, however, remained bound by the historical context of their societies in their respective analyses. During their time, the nineteenth century for the former and the turn of this century for the latter, production considerations, industrialization and factory life still dominated society. Therefore, their view of the role of systems of meaning in society remained tied to the relative functioning of the production process. Only Marx was aware of the "realization problem" of capital, since his analysis of the capitalist system was the most extensive of the two, but neither he nor Weber thought much about the importance of symbolic elements to the solution of that problem. As Baudrillard has pointed out, Marx did not fathom the ultimate and perhaps central role that consumption would play in the maturation of the capitalist system during the 20th century.

To be fair to Weber, his stratification scheme for society emphasized the same factor as Marx, namely *wealth;* but he added to it the factor of *prestige* or *status,* basing it largely on symbolic and cultural concerns. As time went on, the role of status and its symbolic components became increasingly important in the social world of capitalism. This is especially true once the transformation to a consumer society began to take place during the early part of the twentieth century. The lifestyle of the wealthy and the commodities characterizing it, such as large homes, fancy cars, and fashionable designer clothing became prestige items or objects of desire as the culture shifted to the norm of consumption. It was left for others—people like Thorstein Veblen, for example, rather than Weber—to draw out the full implications that the relatively independent role of status considerations would play in the dynamics of capitalist society.

Status Considerations and the Early Consumer Society

Members of the early Protestant sects that Weber recognized as possessing the strongest affinity to capitalist functional requirements were aesthetes. Men wore plain clothes that consisted of a white shirt, black jacket and pants. Women covered their heads and wore a similar black dress and white blouse. They eschewed all types of so-called frivolous purchases and lived plainly. They neither smoked nor drank. It was precisely these and other practices, sanctioned by religious ideas, which made them so able to accumulate capital. Early-rising, long work days at the sites of commerce, and Scrooge-like running of the business were the secrets of success for these capitalists. In particular, the way of life of the protestant aesthetes differed markedly from the more affluent class of the time, namely, the landed aristocracy. The latter lived in ostentatious splendor on country estates. Their progeny often moved to the city where they indulged in all kinds of frivolous displays of wealth, such as the style of living known as the "dandy" or "flaneur." As practiced by aristocratic men during the 18th century, the life of the dandy, involved dressing flamboyantly, pursuing women, especially the wives of wealthy capitalists, sleeping late, and never, never working for a living.

In the social world of early capitalism, then, consumption played a limited role. The key activity was manufacture or business and the accumulation of capital. The landed aristocracy sat on the industrial sidelines while struggling to maintain their *political* dominance of society, and could only watch as the rural populace moved in great numbers to the cities and the sites of industrial manufacture thus depleting the aristocracy's ability to produce agricultural goods and replenish its wealth.

By the late 1800s, industrial capitalism had become the most formidable economic system on the planet. It had thoroughly transformed England, was changing the structure of European society on the continent, especially in France and Germany, and, due in part to the manufacturing needs of warfare during the Civil War, was transforming American society as well. As the shift to capitalism became more prevalent in all western societies, the vanguard of change was composed, not of the aesthetic Protestant sects studied by Weber, but by the burgeoning numbers of upper-middle-class business people, or the "nouveau riches." This group, which became the capitalist class, looked to the landed aristocracy and its ostentatious lifestyle for its status signifiers.

As mentioned previously, Thorstein Veblen wrote the classic work on the lifestyle of the affluent at the turn of the century (1899). Consumerism was a privilege of that class, but had not progressed beyond aping the aristocracy. To show their social status, the affluent purchased large country homes dedicated to conspicuous consumption and mimicked the social conventions of the landed gentry with country clubs, debutante balls, dinner parties, frivolous purchasing of "objets d'art," Paris fashions for the ladies, and the employment of servants, gardeners, and game wardens.

The country mansions of the 19th century established the suburban norm of high status that remains as a desirable sign system. Wealthy owners dedicated the front of the home to a large expanse of land left to worthless lawn grass and an expansive driveway. The lawn, in particular, required hours of landscaping labor for it to retain its symbolic state of productive idleness. Suburban estates of the affluent had many more rooms than necessary to bed and service the immediate household. They reserved the excess space for weekend guests or used it simply as a symbol of ostentatious idleness, like the front lawn. Estates had separate dining and living rooms used by conspicuous consumers on special occasions, while everyday activities occurred in conveniently placed parlors or family rooms. Finally, wealthy owners landscaped the backyards of these houses as gardens and recreational areas. Backyard games such as croquet, badminton, and lawn tennis were popular during the nineteenth century. Each of these housing and land-use elements joined in a system of signs that signified status and wealth. They characterize suburban housing even today. Normative homes in surburban areas throughout the country have separate dining and living room areas, an idle, ostentatious front lawn, and a backyard dedicated to leisure.

We could not characterize society, at this time, as a themed environment. Recourse to thematic elements in the organization of life was restricted to the relatively small class of capitalists who pursued almost single-mindedly the theme of aristocratic ostentation as conspicuous consumption. In contrast, the overwhelming majority of people in the United States remained relatively poor workers employed in factories at low wages who could not afford much in the way of consumer goods save the necessities of food, clothing, and shelter. As workers, they possessed a low social status signified by their lack of money and their social separation from the world of middle-class activities in such things as education, art, family celebrations, and leisure.

Thus, by the 1920s, U.S. capitalism remained dominated by considerations of production and manufacturing, while the symbolic universe of consumption developed only in limited ways and remained populated by the select group of successful middle-class businesspeople and their families. The principal theme guiding consumption was the concerted aping, by the capitalists, of the landed aristocracy and their prestige symbols. Between the years of 1920 and 1950, however, several forces emerged which began to transform the entire society into one organized around the process of consumption and laid the foundation for the themed consumer society of today. Among these forces were,

1. the shift to what is called "Fordism" in industry,
2. the growth of a lower middle class and home consumption activities organized around the theme of modernism that is also associated with Fordism,
3. the uncontrolled societal breakdown during the Great Depression, and
4. the emergence of a mass advertising industry.

Each of these aspects, in their own way, transformed capitalism to a system with a different social structure than that of the past, and with that change caused both the increasing economic emphasis on consumption and the use of themes in organizing everyday culture.

The Advent of Fordism

In the United States, capitalist social organization reached impressive heights by the beginning of the 20th century. We possessed a rich agricultural hinterland that provided an abundance of food and used advanced industrial techniques of farming including American inventions like McCormick's reaper. We had a large labor force continually replenished by immigrants who adjusted well to the long hours of the factory regimen. Finally, in the early 1900s we had an expanding mass of developed land that allowed for the growth of cities, towns, and villages, including new opportunities at every intersection for creative business ideas and enterprises. Industrial society had developed to the point where businesses could produce an immense quantity of goods including clothing and machinery, using mass assembly line techniques. In this innovation of factory organization, individual craft manufacture was replaced by the piecemeal assembly of goods in mass quantities by breaking down each operation, training personnel to do only one part of the whole assembly process and then arranging each group of trained personnel and their specific tasks on a long assembly line. As the raw material of commodities passed from one work station to another, the goods were assembled part by part until workers at the end of the line finished the product and made it ready for consumer purchase. Within Fordist factories each laborer could produce a mass of goods in this manner.

The innovation of the mass assembly line, which Adam Smith had already observed evolving in the pin manufacture of 18th century England, resulted in an explosion of commodity production. Mass quantities of relatively complicated producer goods such as boilers, sewing machines, and farm equipment, and consumer goods such as electrical appliances and clothing became readily available. The abundance of producer goods meant even more success for American capitalism, because it enabled greater amounts of products to be produced. As previously discussed, however, the presence of consumer goods presents capitalism with a dilemma, the "realization problem," because unless the goods can be sold, capital will not realize a profit on their manufacture. Industrial workers were still paid relatively little, because that was an historical condition for the accumulation of profits.

The dilemma facing capitalism was very straight forward. How could the economy move in the necessary direction of producing mass quantities of consumer goods if the average worker could not afford them? The U.S. economy was poised, after World War I, at a point of great opportunity for expansion because of its developed manufacturing infrastructure of factories and its large population of disciplined workers. But it had nowhere to go, except toward deep crisis, without an increase in the ability of workers to afford the fruits of their own labor.

Perhaps the most dynamic solution to this problem was offered by the accomplished entrepreneur, Henry Ford. Ford did not invent the motor car, but he single-handedly perfected its manufacture. He used mass assembly line techniques, selectively picked his industrial workers, and combined the two in large factories that could make mass quantities of cars. After the success of the "Model T" car, introduced in 1908 and purchased largely by the affluent middle class, Ford aimed a new production model at a more modest market price level. This "Model A" was meant to be a car for the masses. However, since the masses could not afford one on their salaries, Ford was presented with a dilemma—our now familiar realization problem. According to Aglietta (1979) and Gramsci (1994), Ford and other capitalists of his time solved that problem by increasing the salaries of their workers, although there are other accounts of why wages were raised (see Chamberlain 1965, pp. 134–145). Ford believed that mass assembly would work if the large quantities of consumer products it produced were affordable. By raising the wages of his workers Ford hoped to create a mass market for his own product. He also urged other capitalists to follow suit, so that the society itself would move in the direction of greater consumption levels.

The use of advanced manufacturing techniques, such as time-motion studies, the mass assembly line and the social mechanisms of improving the purchasing power of workers became known as *Fordism*. The term was first coined by the Marxist philosopher, Antonio Gramsci, in the 1930s but popularized by the French political economist, Michel Aglietta, (1979) in an influential analysis of twentieth century capitalism's success. Fordism, and Henry Ford's enterprise in particular, was remarkably successful. As Ford hoped, many other large-scale manufacturers across the country followed his example and raised their worker's wages. Workers were happier because they were earning more and could afford to buy more products; capitalists were happier because they were using the productive capacity of their mass assembly factories; and the society prospered and expanded in influence because of the greater wealth it held. Rather than dependency on an export-oriented economy, Fordism allowed countries to expand and develop by creating domestic markets for their goods. The key to success was the transformation of workers living at bare levels of subsistence to ones with more disposable income due to higher salaries and their reshaping into voracious consumers.

The American romance with the automobile, which followed on the success of Fordism, almost singlehandedly gave birth to several thematic elements that are the foundations for the so-called "American way of life." Manufacturers advertised automobiles vigorously because people in this country had to be convinced to buy one for leisure reasons. Horses remained popular as modes of transportation for business deliveries and even

During the 1950s, modernist streamlining of automobile design merged with jet fighter forms to produce cars with futuristic fins, such as the Plymouth Fury depicted in the photograph. Photo courtesy of Corbis-Bettmann.

for trolley commuter traffic within cities. Advertisements for cars appealed to the "freedom" of the open road, the excitement and comfort of automobile travel, and, not the least, the status of owning your own car as a differentiating factor among individuals in society. The private car was simultaneously a sign of success and progress—a dual signifier.

In short, once Fordism succeeded in making the automobile available to the consumer masses, new thematic elements were introduced through advertising. They include the attractive images of travel as freedom, of mechanical means as superior to other modes of transportation or consumption, of progress and the abandonment of a horse-drawn traditional life. By pushing the mass purchasing of automobiles, Fordism was also responsible for creating a new object of desire in the minds of the masses. The private car was a mechanical marvel, a sign of progress, of status, of freedom, and the new confluence of desire and affordability for consumers. It persists even now as the continual source of consumer thematic fantasies through advertising and the fashion of commodity changes—the link between the car and the consumer has not diminished in its intensity of desire over the last seventy years.

Household Consumption and Modernism

At the turn of the century most people's homes were sparsely furnished affairs, reflecting their limited purchasing power. This was true whether individuals lived in city tenements or on rural farms. Furnishings were largely heirlooms, hand-me-downs, or custom-built objects. As the number of middle-class people in the United States increased, however, new commodities destined for home use became more apparent. The household was the domain of the woman, as it is to a certain extent today, and many manufacturers aimed their products at her needs. During the nineteenth century, household living arrangements were little different than they had been for thousands of years. Women's domestic chores were labor intensive. Washing, cooking, and cleaning were done by hand, utilizing wood or coal fires and backbreaking tools such as the washboard, mops, and brooms. Advertising for early industrial products designed for home consumption such as the hand cranked washing machine or the foot-operated sewing machine, trumpeted their value as laborsaving devices. They were promoted as a new norm of household organization.

The department store catalogues that appeared in the nineteenth century were perhaps the most powerful of the early innovations that led to the creation of a thematic environment. They included everything from mass-produced farm machinery to clothing (such as suits of any size) and labor saving household appliances. The famous Sears Roebuck catalog, for example, contained hand-drawn illustrations of consumer products along with advertising copy promoting these goods as objects of desire. The catalogues reached millions of American homes that, for the first time, were subjected to the kinds of thematic appeals characteristic of commodity advertising. In particular, the early mail order catalogues were responsible for converting industrial goods into an *image*. The image was born out of necessity because of the nature of mail order marketing. Yet, once it took its place alongside advertising copy (written appeals that promote and enjoin consumers to buy a product), the consumer universe of desire was driven by images and representations that tapped into cognitive associations that were pure symbols. The thematic environment began to emerge from this context. Desire was fueled not only by the images or the copy but also by the juxtaposition between image and copy—a powerful feature characteristic of advertising today, as Roland Barthes (1993) observed (see the next chapter).

During the early twentieth century the invention of electrical appliances by people like Edison coupled with the taming of electricity by Nichola Tesla combined to open a vast domain of commodities destined for home use. Household appliances became electrified. Refrigerators replaced ice boxes; sewing machines, vacuum cleaners, and washing machines appeared as the cornerstones of the new commodified household. Their manufacture, by virtue of the mass assembly techniques of Fordism, became the backbone of the expanding industrial enterprise of peace time American capitalism. General Electric, Westinghouse, Singer and Electrolux took their places next to the emerging giants of automobile manufacture—Ford, General Motors,

During the 1950s, with the mass production of suburban living, housewives were targeted by the modernist ideal of the all-electric kitchen. Photo courtesy of Corbis-Bettmann.

and Chrysler—as major "blue-chip" corporations. The larger the middle class grew, the more capitalism developed as a consumer-oriented economy, and that in turn, produced the wealth that increased even more the size of the middle-class consumer market.

Mass Consumerism and Design

In Europe, during the early 1900s, as we have discussed in Chapter 2, several distinguished architects and designers worked together to push a reaction against the eclecticism of haphazard Victorian Era design as a unified, geometrically-based concept called "modernism." Industrial producers applied the modernist design methodology not only to the largest structures (that is, buildings and city planning) but also to the most intimate spaces of interior home furnishings. Modernism stressed clean designs that lacked symbolic appeals, as we have already seen. The most important aspect of the movement was its unity of vision that encompassed the entire spectrum of consumerism. As exemplified best in the works of the German Bauhaus design center during the 1920s, modernist designers re-formed every piece of home furnishings from kitchens and their appliances, to living rooms and their furniture to bedrooms, and, even, to the outside facades of homes. This *unity* of design principles from the inside to the outside was a distinguishing feature of modernism (see Lefebvre 1974). In brief, modernist design created an entirely new and consistently orchestrated home environment, which was also thematically linked to the design practices outside the home that were producing the skyscraper concentrations in the industrial city.

In transforming the newly designed surroundings, modernist culture also transformed the themes of consumer society. The movement was most associated with the ideas of "progress," technological efficiency, functionality of design, and the concept of the "ensemble," (the concordant appearance of one object with another). The promotion of modernist designs changed the nature of advertising, especially those ads directed at homemakers. By the 1920s the themes that were stressed involved technological progress and the fashion to "be modern," electrical and mechanical wizardry in the home, and the high status of newness. These themes were played out in the burgeoning business of advertising. It used the new, emergent forms of the mass media, such as radio and magazines in addition to the now classic catalogue merchandising. Radio program sponsors that manufactured soap combined their efforts with those that built washing machines to entice listening housewives to consume the latest products in the interest of being modern. By the 1920s, the consumer society was characterized by: a mass market of workers turned consumers, the commodification of the household and housing through modernism, the increasing use of the private car, the rise and powerful influence of the mass media, especially radio and magazines, the explosive growth of the advertising industry, and, the production of fantasies creating the desire for objects through a thematic environment.

Finally, as I discussed in Chapter 2, the creation of a mass market for domestic life, including the shift to suburbia, produced a change in the role of adult women from that of houseworker to home manager. Women became the target for the creation of new needs that were basic to the Fordist economy, which included sectors producing electrified manufactured goods in mass quantities. Yet, as our emphasis on the problematic nature of capital realization suggests, compliance to the new marketing appeals by middle class women were not automatic. It was necessary for corporations to create a mass market for their wares. Specific advertising appeals to housewives through the mass media accomplished the task. As Roger Miller (1990) points out, one significant influence in this social shift was the 1929 book of Christine Frederick called *Selling Mrs. Consumer*. Frederick was a disciple of the Fordist regulatory ideology propagated by Frederick Winslow Taylor, mentioned previously, otherwise known as "Taylorism," and she had adapted his "scientific management" techniques to the home environment. Christine Frederick argued in her book that corporations producing domestic commodities should not view housewives as a monolithic market. Instead, they should treat them as market segmentations with each receptive to differentiated advertising appeals (Miller 1990:4). Along with this shift was the need, according to Frederick, to appeal more to images than the intrinsic use-value of the new, laborsaving commodities. According to Miller,

> She advised advertisers to appeal to the less logical, more emotional aspects of female psychology, while at the same time educating women into the use of the new products of domestic technology. The strategies employed by Madison Avenue to exploit the new domestic market radically altered earlier practices utilized in different types of ad campaigns. Advertisements that previously had extolled the intrinsic quality, durability, and rich detail of products began to associate consumer goods with idealized images of lifestyle. After ideal roles had been promoted in media of sufficient circulation to assure their acceptance as general norms, it was relatively easy to create feelings of inferiority and guilt in women who fell short of them. . . . These feelings of personal inadequacy could be translated into consumer 'needs,' an explicitly ideological manipulation based on distorted forms of information exchange (1990:5).

A similar process in the direction of advertising appeals also occurred for other kinds of products and mass markets (Ewen 1976; Williamson 1978; Goldman 1994). Such changes laid the ground work for a truly qualitative shift in consumer mores after 1930. Prior to that time, products appealed to people because of their potential use-value. After the 1930s, the consumers' desire for new commodities focused on their image or symbolic value. I shall return to this important observation later.

The Great Depression

Another change in American society occurred during the late 1920s that eventually sealed the fate of our formerly thrifty and subsistent society and erased all alternate lifestyles that had previously remained untouched by consumerism either through lack of money or by choice of values. That event was the Great Depression and its subsequent slow restructuring of our society in the 1930s did not really stabilize until the late 1940s.

The spectacular and most commonly associated feature of the depression, the horrendous crash of stocks on Wall Street in 1929, has been explained often as the failure of the investment institution to safeguard against overextended purchasing and the availability of too-easy credit. However, the real damage to the country, and, we may add, the western world of capitalism, was not only the fateful events of 1929 but the subsequent years when capitalism recovered at a level that had adjusted to mass unemployment, the frequent failure of farms and small banks, a timid stock market, and a no-growth Gross National Product. During the early 1930s the slide toward economic ruin by U.S. capitalism had been halted but at such a low level of business activity that financial disaster for most of the people was simply institutionalized.

Consequently, when people spoke about "recovery" in the 1930s they were not referring to preventing a further crash on Wall Street, but to rejuvenating the economy to its former robust level. The voters realized this issue was political, because they viewed the government as able to play a role in revitalizing the economy, and so they elected the Democratic administration of Franklin Roosevelt, who promised government's help. The ideas that emerged to help explain the nation's predicament and to guide its economic resurgence were articulated in England by the economist John Maynard Keynes, although the crisis of capitalism was both explained and predicted by the socialist economist, M. Kalecki, several years before. As Keynes argued, there was nothing intrinsic within a competitive capitalist system that led it to stabilize around high levels of growth or employment. Once business failures were cleaned out in every sector, the economy could function without disaster for many years at a *low* level of activity. To be sure, in this latter case, most people would be unemployed and most businesses would be bankrupt. However, Keynes showed that these effects did not mean the destruction of capitalism, only its survival with a smaller productive capacity. In brief, Keynes implied that the social effects of depression could be with the country for a long time, while the down-scaled economy would "prosper" in its own manner.

Keynes suggested that if a society wished to move away from this low equilibrium level of economic activity, it could not rely on the private sector itself. Government had to step in and, as a matter of policy, increase public spending in a way that stimulated the expansion of the economy. This analysis and its public policy implications became the cornerstone for the Roosevelt administration's recovery plan. Simply put, the government began to spend so that more people would have money to spend. That, it was hoped, would stimulate business and eventually lead to a higher level of economic activity and ultimately more taxes that could make up the losses in government spending. The private sector viewed the government as a "pump-priming" mechanism for the economy. It would spend money and go into debt, but it would so stimulate the economy that, in time, more people would be working and more goods and services would be produced. An increase in economic activity would, in turn, lead to greater tax revenues being collected and being available to service the debt. In Keynesian policies, government spending leads to increases in private wealth which then lead to increasing tax revenues that then covers government spending and debt. Some Americans believed this claim to be a trick. Many others believed it to be true and supported government recovery policies.

One critical aspect of anti-depression government spending was public policy aimed at putting more money in the hands of workers. If jobs were not available from the private sector, they would be created by the public sector. The unemployed would receive unemployment insurance that maintained their household revenue for a time, and, if people could not afford consumer goods, they could tap into forms of easy credit sponsored by the federal government. With these and other measures, public policy provided people with more money in the hope that they would both spend and save more and, by that, stimulate businesses and banks. Part of the new thrust associated with economic recovery from the depression, therefore, relied heavily on consumerism. At the height of the depression, people who were making a salary either through public or private means were enjoined to spend and purchase to do their share in the recovery effort.

This period in our history has had a lasting effect in changing a norm of our society from one of frugality or saving to one of consumerism and debt-financed household spending. Through the stimulation of credit-based buying, especially in the housing market, people for the first time could go into debt without social stigma. The society viewed debt-financed consumption as good for the economy, because that was seen as the means of stimulating business. Furthermore, government programs made it attractive to go into debt. Banking acts of Congress that were passed to stimulate the economy made the interest on loans for homes and automobiles tax deductible. In particular, deductibility from taxes was a consumer incentive meant to boost the banking, automobile and housing industries, but it also made borrowing to purchase homes and cars attractive.

Before the 1930s the "norm of saving" dominated consumer culture. People earned little and they viewed their lives as a long process by which they would work hard, live frugally and, eventually, have enough savings to get married, raise a family and, perhaps, buy a home. After the 1930s Americans were acculturated to the "norm of consumption" (Aglietta 1979) that encouraged people to spend and go into debt because of easy credit and the disappearance of the stigma attached to borrowing, since the loans were typically financed or sponsored by the federal government and were directly associated with the economic recovery from the depression. By the late 1930s, at the time World War II broke out, many Americans were eager to obtain loans for the purchase of automobiles and single-family homes. The auto and home-building industries were leading the way out of the depression. We will never know if Keynes' policies and the Roosevelt administration's ideas would have eventually succeeded, because the outbreak of World War II, and the U.S. involvement in that war, became the single greatest Keynesian opportunity of that time. It led to government spending amounting to billions of dollars and the creation of millions of new jobs in support of the war effort.

No matter what sparked the depression recovery, however, a transformed culture remained after the 1940s where people adapted to the norm of consumption and eagerly anticipated going into debt to finance the purchase of cars and homes. By the 1950s, the nation of savers had become a nation of consumers, and consumption had become a new American ideal that fueled the fantasy appeals of advertising (Galbraith 1978).

The Mass Advertising Industry

The economic needs of depression recovery that included a switch to consumer debt-financing and the economic need to stimulate consumption to solve the realization problem of capital are not the same needs. However, they worked together in a completely complementary way to create a nation of active consumers. Permissible norms pushed the ability to consume beyond the margins of individual resources and included, by the 1950s, the acceptability of debt-financed household consumption. At the turn of the century the mere acquisition of a loan was socially stigmatized. By the 1950s loans were commonplace and going into debt to finance a home was no longer shocking, but was now conventional. Government programs eased consumer credit and created millions of new consumers through acts that facilitated the transition of returning veterans to civilian life. The series of acts known as the GI Bill, for example, made it possible for veterans to purchase a new home with as little as one dollar down.

As millions of people shifted to a high-consumption lifestyle, the advertising industry also shifted into high gear. It became the general purveyor of consumer fantasies and themes for the nation. I have already noted how important was the shift of advertising to the mass media outlets, especially magazines and radio. The use of the mass media by advertising and its positioning as the principal means by which commodities such as cars and home furnishings were promoted resulted in the growth of advertising companies into a major American industry. By the early 1950s this industry was located principally in the area of Manhattan on Madison Avenue above 42nd street. From these offices that eventually employed thousands of people specialized in copywriting, art direction, and even marketing psychology, professional practices were brought to bear on the production of consumer fantasies, the promotion of desire for commodities, and the manipulation of market demand for the sake of individual products.

American capitalism under Fordist arrangements had worked well in creating the conditions for a mass consumer market. By the 1950s, however, that same system was comprised of corporate producers who competed with each other in every industry. While it was true that most sectors of the economy were controlled by a few firms, that is, most sectors were *oligopolies,* and not either freely competitive nor monopolies, considerable competition remained among oligopolistic corporations for market share. This struggle for the consumer dollar was enjoined principally through advertising and superficial marketing ploys because the basic products remained quite similar. For example, the "big four" dominated the automobile industry during the 1950s (to become the "big three" by the 1970s, plus Japan and Germany). Ford, Chrysler, General Motors and American Motors manufactured most cars, though other, smaller companies such as Studebaker and Hudson existed then. Each of these manufacturers produced similar types of cars—sedans, coupes, station wagons, and convertibles—for the private consumer market. Corporate brands and car names—not the features of construction—made the difference between consumer choices.

Consumers, for example, could purchase a specific model and have a choice of a six- or eight-cylinder engine, an automatic or manual transmission, and, for some types of cars, either a two- or a four-door model. Beyond the basic structural differences, however, consumer choices were also extended to more superficial distinctions in cars. First, for each manufacturer, models were divided in a completely superficial way among separate car divisions. Ford was split among Ford, Mercury, and Lincoln dealers; Chrysler had Dodge, Plymouth, and Chrysler divisions. General Motors hyperdifferentiated its products into separated lines based loosely on perceived price differences—Chevrolet, Buick, Cadillac, and Oldsmobile—each of which appeared as different divisions. Second, cars competed with each other through differences in colors, trim, and design (the 1950s was famous for its fin wars). Third, although engines and transmissions were virtually similar, manufacturers gave cars different names and promoted them as competitively superior.

Using newspapers, magazines, radio, and, later, television, manufacturers aggressively marketed these differences to consumers. As big as the American corporations became during the 1950s and 1960s so did their respective advertising budgets increase. Advertising became a multibillion dollar a year industry and its companies branched out to offices in Chicago, Kansas City, St. Louis, Los Angeles and San Francisco. The intense competition among producers selling products that differed little from each other led to the increasingly intense plumbing of the depths of American culture for themes and images to which appeals could be made. The power of advertising, its unswerving pressure to create modes of desire in the individual consumer, and its relentless scouring of the American psyche for symbolically meaningful appeals formed the foundation for the themed environment of the present.

Early home market catalogues used copy to describe in as much detail as possible the advantages of using specific products. As I suggested above, early appeals were made to the use-value of commodities. This attention to specifications and utility became the principal mode of mass advertising. By the 1950s, following the Fordist marketing transformations of the 1930s, advertising had progressed beyond the specification of use-value to promote the image itself as a sign either of fashion or progress, or occasionally both. If all cars were pretty much the same, why would a consumer seek to buy a new car? Appeals were made less about the use-value of a new car than about the value of "newness" itself. The "fin wars" of the 1950s erupted because cars were being differentiated by advertising according to their appearance and not by virtue of advantages in technological innovations. As the previous discussion of advertising aimed at the housewife also showed, this process operated in the domestic appliance market as well. In brief, by the 1950s, the multibillion dollar advertising industry had shifted from informing the consumer about the use-value of products to the *manipulation* of the consumer, using symbolic or image-dependent appeals.

Another characteristic of the emergence of mass advertising was that people imported its methods into other important areas of American life, because its techniques of manipulation had become so successful. One clear example was in the realm of politics. Before the 1950s campaigns were waged through the traditional means of voter organization by parties and "machines" and by the rhetorical competition among candidates who went to considerable length to get exposure for themselves in an era dependent on trains and radio. With the elections of 1960 it became apparent that politicians were turning to Madison Avenue for persuasive techniques and basing some of their appeals less on rhetorical debates or ideological differences than on manufactured distinctions promulgated by advertising agencies. It was not by accident that books exposing this process began to appear, such as *The Selling of the President, The Hidden Persuaders*, and *The Image*. As a prelude to the appearance of a themed environment, the manipulative techniques of mass advertising spilled out to other social realms and began to dominate their processes of distinction as well. The activity of "selling" someone or oneself, of "marketing" a person or idea, of "advertisements for oneself," and so on, began to control the logic of social relations in a variety of social spheres that were formerly based on the intrinsic self-worth of people and/or ideas, such as in the area of politics, careers, and science.

When the philosopher Baudrillard criticizes 19th century political economists for focusing on the production process as the key organizing practice of society, he does so by re-affirming the above shift in the importance of advertising. The rule of the image over substance, of appearance over use-value, of manipulation over rhetoric and logic, all derive from the central role that the advertising industry plays in American life. It is a consequence of capital's need to realize wealth under oligopolistic production constraints with little actual differences among products. This substantive change coupled with the structural shifts that occurred in society as a consequence of adjustments to depression-era realities. Those shifts included the adoption of a role for government in promoting the "norm of consumption," the creation of a consumer consciousness among the working class, the commodification of our environment (including the commodification of the home), and the creation of ubiquitous social institutions for mass advertising and mass marketing. Along with structural changes came new sensibilities, such as the personal transformations in the self toward consumption as a domain of self-realization or the shift from housewife (domestic work) to home manager among middle class women.

Currently, we live in a society much different from the world of industrial capitalism that existed prior to the 1950s. Movement toward a themed environment has progressed in sequence with the development of consumerist values and their respective social institutions such as advertising, mass marketing the rise of mass media and the transformed role of the organized labor-capitalist relation. In the next chapter I shall examine closely the nature of this themed environment that consists of a multileveled relationship between the restructuring national economy and a themed culture propelled primarily by the operation of symbols or images, rather than the intrinsic use-value of material objects.

FOUR

The Themed Culture and Themed Environments

From Sales to Marketing: The Themed Culture

In the nineteenth century laborers worked in factories that manufactured commodities. They earned a subsistence wage that was just enough to cover the necessities of life, expressed as a bare minimum of food, clothing and shelter. They had no insurance, retirement funds, or opportunities to send their children to college so they could better themselves. Today our social circumstances have greatly changed. As we have seen, during the twentieth century, economic measures to avoid depression, government policies that prop up consumer spending, and the emergence of a commodity-oriented mass culture helped along by ubiquitous advertising have combined to produce profound social shifts that make us all eager consumers. Today most workers are *relatively* better paid compared to the nineteenth century world of subsistence wages. Yet there remains a big difference between the so-called "working poor" who have considerable burdens in rent, family expenses, medical, insurance, and transportation costs, and the up-scale middle class who own a home, have a car, possess retirement and insurance plans at work, and who can plan to pay for their children's higher education.

Writing in the nineteenth century, Karl Marx believed all industrial workers were exploited. They sold their creative energies for a wage that they then exchanged to purchase their meager commodities. Marx maintained that this exchange was one of individual creativity from the laborer for a subsistence minimum of food and manufactured objects from the employer. Therefore, Marx felt the worker was exploited. He also viewed the exchange relation of labor for a wage in the production of commodities as *alienating* to people. The world of "things," according to Marx dominated the world of work and resulted in the degrading of human labor to a mere thing itself.

Today, however, circumstances are considerably different. A large segment of the U.S. population works in service-information processing industries. Creativity, or the human quality of achieving fulfillment in labor, is a principal way that many employees and employers evaluate these kind of jobs. Most often this takes the form of surveys of client or customer satisfaction, but it also involves the evaluation and transformation of work by credentialed professionals who find fulfillment in careers.

The relatively well-paid segment of society purchases services and commodities without serious financial hardship, because they have been acculturated into accepting debt for lifestyle pursuits. They value customer satisfaction and the realization of self through commodity purchases as much or more than self-realization at the place of work. In today's society, unlike the earlier stages of capitalism (including the period of factory exploitation observed by Marx), the creative power of workers in the "post-industrial" industries is exchanged for the creative power of other workers whose job it is to please them. This relation exists also for the case of commodity purchasing from stores that value customer satisfaction. Thus, while nineteenth century capitalism was dominated by a world of things that held power over "alienated" workers, the present period finds people in a post-industrial world where their creativity is exchanged for commodities that are increasingly acquired for the kind of self-realization that overcomes conditions of exploitation or alienation.

Change on this order, from a societal culture of producers to a culture of consumers does not, however, mean that exploitation has disappeared as part of the employee-employer relation. On the contrary, exploitation persists as the core connection between salaried employees of all kinds and their employers (Mayer 1994) and comprises part of the value of all commodities. This link can most graphically be illustrated in other areas of the globe where manufacturing still takes place under conditions very similar to those of the last century. Exploitation also characterizes the relation between employers and salaried professionals such as physicians, engineers, and professors that do not have profit-sharing arrangements as a condition of their employment. In short, the concept of worker "exploitation" is still relevant, but it has been refined to account for the new realities of our present lives (Mayer 1994). Furthermore, whereas Marx wrote about the problem of alienation as produced by the work relation, our society seems to have overshadowed Marx's dilemma. Alienation is rarely discussed today as a structural problem of society, in the terms that Marx and Marxism once framed the issue (Geyer 1996).

The most pressing problem in today's economy is less one of exploitation or alienation through either work or consumer purchasing and more of how to constantly satisfy primed consumer desires with items that people will want to purchase in mass quantities. This is so because people differentiate among competing suppliers less in terms of the use-value of commodities than according to their ability to assuage some desire created through effective marketing and advertising. As indicated in previous chapters, symbolic processes control the latter value, especially through the desire for status, fashion, sex appeal, or power. In short, by the 1970s capitalism established the structural solution for the profit-realization problem and also successfully deindustrialized, using global locations for manufacturing. These structural changes also altered consumer behavior to demand frequent purchases of goods and buying at unprecedented levels. The new consumer culture requires ever-new fantasies and modes of desire to simply maintain its high level of spending.

In the previous chapter I discussed how the emergence of mass advertising fuels the spending activities of our society through the production of desire. This activity is only one aspect of creating a mass consumer culture. Advertising must be coupled with efficient and timely marketing techniques. Marketing procedures encompass not only the appeals made by advertising, such as those found on television or in magazines, but also appeals within the built environment itself—that is, in the suburb and city-scapes, or the stores and malls that remain responsible for the realization of capital. The key economic relation of the consumer society is not the exchange of money for goods as it was in the nineteenth century, but the link between the promotion of desire in the mass media and advertising, and the commercial venues where goods and services can be purchased.

Store environments today are but an extension of television, magazine, and newspaper advertising. They provide material spaces for the realization of consumer fantasies primed by movies, rock videos, the record industry, commercial advertising, lifestyle orientations from religious, ethnic, racial, or class origins, and even political ideologies that are propagated in community discourse or at the place of work. The built environment operates not only as the fuel for consumer fantasies but also as the spaces within which mass marketing and purchasing takes place. For this reason, the creation of themed environments as the envelope of commercial activity helps resolve the central economic concern regarding the link between commercial venues and our themed culture that is supersaturated by symbols or images.

Marketing Practice

The practice of marketing in the United States has gone from a rather straightforward affair involving the *distribution* of goods to potential customers that existed as a generic mass, otherwise known as "sales," to a knowledge-based, purposeful effort at controlling consumer buying through scientific methods and management techniques. This activity is more commonly called marketing since, unlike sales, companies target it toward specific consumer groups. Not too long ago, for example, many products were sold through door-to-door traveling salespeople, with little thought about the different types of consumers they might encounter. Among other goods, this activity included the selling of brushes, cosmetics, encyclopedias, household appliances such as vacuum cleaners, and, at the turn of the century, phonograph players.

While the once ubiquitous "Fuller Brush Man" has passed into urban history, communities around the country are still hosts to traveling "Avon Ladies" or Mary Kay cosmetics sales people. Marketing as sales once consisted of such peripatetic devices along with the artfully designed catalogues that were mass mailed to homes. The sales pitch was based on a direct appeal to a relatively undifferentiated mass audience through oral or written discourse centering on the demonstrable use-value of individual products. Avon ladies or vacuum cleaner sales people, for example, went into homes to demonstrate their products, that is, they personally exhibited commodity use-value.

As consumer affluence increased, especially after World War II, and large department stores and other commercial establishments appeared, which catered to local customers, the need to travel door to door declined. In addition, as we have already discussed, appeals using *symbolic* values or the production of images of desire progressively replaced appeals to the use-value of commodities. Marketing, rather than sales, began to dominate the business enterprise, because of the recurrent crises in the realization of capital—not the least of which was the Great Depression, as we have seen. Even the designers and planners of products, that is, those people who once led the production process of manufacturing and represented the projection of a product's future, worked closely with company employees in charge of marketing. The placement of the realization problem of capital at the center of business concerns, rather than labor or manufacturing issues per se, has also resulted in the rise of marketing as the principal aspect of corporate administration.

Marketing employs sophisticated psychological techniques aimed at promoting desire, the manipulation of consumer needs, art and design aimed at the production of appealing environments and packaging, demographic analysis that identifies clusters of potential consumers, and advertising specialists that have replaced the door-to-door or catalogue sales people with highly refined techniques of ad production and distribution. As many observers have noted, marketing procedure today slices apart the mass of consumers into individual "market segments" or clusters (Langdon 1994; Weiss 1988), using highly accurate demographic techniques and lifestyle surveys. Advertisers then aim specific appeals at these particular segments. They base the clusters on a range of individual *differences*. These are often arrayed as oppositions, at least during the process of discovery and the production of marketing appeals. These dichotomies include urban versus suburban; married versus singles; working class versus yuppie professionals; ethnics versus multi-generationed Americans; regional distinctions such as the Midwest, the South, the Northeast; populations graded by income brackets distinguished in relatively small increments; racial differences; renter versus homeowner status; age distinctions; life course distinctions, and so on.

According to Michael J. Weiss (1988), a popular target marketing system has divided the U.S. population into 40 separate clusters. These can be found in all geographical areas of the United States and pertain specifically to consumer market types based on aggregate and similar lifestyles. Each market segment has been classified according to tastes in cars, magazines, leisure activities, food, television habits, and preferred commodity purchases. These segments reflect combined factors such as income, education, stage in the life course, family status, urban-suburban location, ethnicity, race, housing status, and other demographic factors. Advertisers target these segments using appeals specifically designed for each cluster, often irrespective of the particular product sold.

The targeting practices of contemporary marketing have given corporations a picture of our national population that consists of diverse lifestyles. Advertisers direct appeals at two levels with two distinct types of products. At one level, they aim marketing efforts at particular segments of the consuming public. Commodities are designed specifically to appeal to these segments. At another level, however, they search for *mass* appeal objects that can cut across segments and realize mass sales. In the record industry, for example, companies market different artists and types of music explicitly for segments—rap, hard rock, soft rock, easy listening, top 40, Latin, romantic, punk, or reggae. However, record companies also search for particular artists or bands that can unite these various segments, such as Elvis, Madonna, Frank Sinatra, or Michael Jackson. It is often said about Madonna, for example, that she continually reinvents herself, hence the basis of her persisting popularity. Madonna is a mass object of consumption. The same thing can*not* be said about rap singers or reggae bands, because they appeal to segmented markets and usually cannot effect cross-segment appeal, although there are exceptions such as Bob Marley or the United Kingdom band UB40 (in the case of reggae), that make it to "top 40" radio play.

The Shift to Market Segmentation

The important shift in marketing to segmentation and its reliance on themes can be illustrated by developments in the suburban housing market. Segmentation is central to the concept of selling suburban homes. Researchers take the U.S. population of potential home buyers and cluster them into several distinct market segments. A slightly different logic of consumption that motivates variation in the style of housing drives each segment. Consequently, marketing campaigns can treat them as separate entities. Yuppies or "young urban professionals," dinks or "double income, no kids," and "sunset community" or developments dedicated to elderly and/or retired people, are terms that have emerged out of the lexicon of marketing in recent years.

This process of market segmentation based on lifestyle clusters results in two distinct outcomes. One the one hand, segmentation leads to the increasing *segregation* of the population by dividing it into evermore restricted homogeneous units (Langdon 1994: 65). On the other, population clustering and competition among developers forces the latter to devise new and relatively unique ways of marketing their products through the creative use of symbols. To the earlier and relatively narrow themes of nineteenth century suburbanization, which principally focused on affluence and status, suburban developers now add the exploitation of a host of thematic devices that derive from consumer fantasies. It is the latter practice, an increasing reliance on fantasies from popular media, that contributes to a landscape dominated entirely by themes.

Marketing considerations, for example, dictated that it was preferable for developments to possess some overarching motif. Most frequently this imperative took the simple form of denotating the development with some catchy name or title, such as "Elysian Fields," "Mountain Estates," or "Harbor Ranch." In this way the advertising niche of a particular project could be established and money devoted to achieving name recognition for the product. Real estate builders sold labeled developments as an aggregate of homes and a location rather than advertising separate buildings.

Often the thematic identification of a development was materially operationalized in landscaping and construction practices. Marketing experts preferred to provide developments with a distinctive signature form of design. Once a theme was chosen, it was carried out as a motif throughout the development. Thus, the planners of the suburban project harmoniously orchestrated its thematic elements. This kind of practice is called "scenography." For example, if a tropical paradise theme were chosen, builders would paint all the houses various shades of Miami pastels. Landscapers would make frequent use of tropical plants, such as the "bird of paradise" or palm trees.

Besides these design elements that are harmonious with the development's overarching theme, scenography practices extend to the entrance of the project. The entranceways for many developments serve to frame the overarching theme of the project. In the example of our tropical paradise, the entrance might be landscaped with lush plants and palm trees surrounding a fountain or simulated, artificially constructed waterfall. In front of this micro environment, developers would locate the carefully chosen name of the development, perhaps "Parrot Cove," "Everglades Estates," "Miami Heights," or "Paradise Manor." In short, the development names, internal design motifs, scenography of landscaping and entrances all aim for thematic unity through homogeneous elements of construction.

As suburbanization has continued in the United States and competition among developers has increased, the need to emphasize thematic aspects of housing has become more crucial to the marketing process. Over the years developers devoted a greater effort to developing and incorporating fantasy elements in suburban housing. However, at rock bottom, the marketing or selling of homes remains grounded in the considerations always present in the desire to obtain suburban residence. The signs of status and wealth continue to prevail, despite the evermore elaborate role that fantasy plays in marketing. Prospective home buyers still most desire to know what the square footage of the home is, how many cars the garage can accommodate, the value of surrounding homes, how stable the area, how good the schools, what occupations and kinds of cars the neighbors have, and so on. Decor and design remain ancillary to the imperatives of exchange value and investment considerations when purchasing expensive items like housing.

Thus, although the process of marketing relies increasingly on fantasy elements, which gives us the themed environment, more standard considerations such as the desire for signs of wealth and prestige that were always characteristic of consumer desires also apply. Themes of fantasy, such as tropical paradise, mountain vistas, or Victorian gentrification, and themes of wealth, luxury, and opulence (despite the long history of the latter in the marketing of suburban location), are not mutually exclusive and are, instead, mutually reinforcing in the consumer culture of the present, where they reappear in a variety of contexts from the construction of hotels and malls to Las Vegas casinos.

The Themed Environment

The domination of marketing considerations above other aspects of commodity production and the increasing use of market segmentation to keep up with a highly differentiated consumer public contributes to the proliferation of themed environments. Themes are direct marketing appeals. They reduce the product to its image and the consumer experience to its symbolic content. The purpose of all commercial places, as we have seen, is the realization of capital—the selling of goods and/or services. These spaces cannot, however, make this function the prime focus of their appeal to potential consumers, because profit-making benefits corporations or commercial retailers alone. Instead, businesses must disguise the instrumental exchange relation of money for a commodity as another relation between commercial place and the consumer.

Our society bathes the consumer purchase in a benevolent light of nurturing and advertised self-fulfillment. In addition, commercial spaces try to entertain while they promote consumption. People *expect* to be entertained by the commercial environment. Perhaps the theme park illustrates this phenomenon best with its mixture of amusement rides, merchandizing outlets and food courts. As some observers have noted (Postman 1985), a focus on the need for entertainment articulates with every aspect of our society, including politics, education, work, and the serious discussion of social issues. With this cultural change has come changes in our expectations that make entertainment a premium of social encounters, thereby reinforcing the saturation of commercialized entertainment throughout our culture.

Thus, the commercial environment, taken as a whole, has increasingly been designed as a sign itself, as some symbolic space that *connotes* something other than its principal function—the realization of capital through the stimulation of consumer desires and the promotion of sales. It provides a form of entertainment while stimulating the transformation of individuals to commodity-craving selves. All establishments dependent on the attraction of paying customers, therefore, have progressively resorted to overarching thematic devices that disguise the space's fundamental purpose with some general motif or theme. The theme not only promises the realization of desire, but also advertises producer "benevolence" through a facade of nurturing that suggests it has the best interests of people at heart. In addition to the production of desire through the connection with mass advertising, the themed environment promotes deals, discounts, rebates, sales, special purchasing arrangements, easy credit, customization, and care that are all part of the seller's marketing strategy for the daily seduction of the consumer.

There are many themed environments in our society. Restaurants divide themselves between specifically promoted images and according to the type of food they serve; museums specialize in particular artifacts and advertise special exhibits with overarching themes; department stores sell symbols along with goods, such as through the use of designer clothing labels; malls adopt general design motifs; and theme parks proliferate as the preferred form of family entertainment. As I have discussed in the last chapter, even the interior of the home was commodified through thematic devices and incorporated into the cyclical sphere of fashion. Some of these themed environments, such as home interiors or restaurants, are designed to be used daily, that is, they are part of our everyday life. Others are meant for special occasions, such as the theme park destination of family vacations or holidays. All of these environments, however, share a common link in the promotion of commercial sales, the blending of entertainment with other cultural experiences, and the melding of material space with the media-scape of television, advertising, movies, cyberspace, and commodity marketing. Let us consider some examples.

In what follows I shall emphasize the function of spaces as themed environments and pay special attention to the symbolic devices used to differentiate otherwise similar commercial places from each other (I have already covered the subject of home interiors). My discussion of motified milieus to follow has two propositions. The first asserts that, due to increased competition among producers and distributors of goods and services, businesses increasingly use themes and symbolic appeals. In the past they relied more on direct demonstrations of the intrinsic use-value of the goods they produced. In the second case, I suggest that, while symbols and motifs were commonly used in the past by commercial establishments to advertise their goods or services, now businesses are increasingly building environments completely designed as themed spaces. These typically consist of some overarching motif complemented by corresponding thematic details throughout the constructed space that together create an entertaining, themed environment. People increasingly enjoy these symbol-filled milieus, such as large malls, for their own sake as entertaining spaces, and not simply as locations for the easy purchase of commodities.

The appearance of such spaces harkens back to earlier history when people lived within environments completely structured by cosmological, religious, or political codes (see Chapter 2). The important difference now is that our themed environments are imitations or *simulations* of substantive symbols. Today's signs possess superficial rather than deeply felt meanings. They are *fundamentally* disconnected from the use-value of the commodities with which they are associated. As pure images, their major source of inspiration is the fickle and rapidly changing fashionable world of mass advertising, television and Hollywood culture. Thus, there is both a positive and a negative side to the proliferation of themed environments. In the former case, they have emerged as a qualitatively new source of entertainment in the history of human civilization. In the latter, their essential purpose of merchandising and profit-making, their control by *private* commercial rather than public interests, and their reduction of all meanings to superficial surface images, compels us to examine closely the significance of the increasingly popular experience they offer. I shall deal in more detail with these pros and cons in the last chapter.

Themed Environments of Everyday Life: Restaurants, Malls, and Airports

The Themed Restaurant

Until quite recently, Americans rarely ate in restaurants. The norm was to cook meals at home. Dining out was reserved for a special occasion. Eating at the local community diner was an exception to this practice, because it offered a substantial breakfast or meat and potatoes dinner for reasonable prices. Frequenters of diners were mainly people on the move, such as truckdrivers, traveling salespeople, delivery men, or single adults, especially bachelors.

The roadside diner was an important place during the 1930s and 1940s, at the first blossoming of our now mature automobile culture. Many of these structures were simple affairs that restricted their advertising to the daily specials (Jakle 1995). They counted on traffic and the sparsity of competition to bring customers their way. Nevertheless, a few of these establishments exploited advertising in competition for business and some managed to develop thematic devices. One classic case was the original McDonald brothers' roadside hamburger stand located in 1955 on Route 66 just west of San Bernardino, California (Cartensen 1995). The brothers embellished their simple diner with a golden logo in the shape of a large "M." Over the years, as the original stand grew into the multi-national, multi-billion dollar corporation under new, franchise thinking owners, this arched logo would undergo many stylistic transformations as it melded with the *theme* of the "McDonald's" experience (Ritzer 1993).

Between 1930 and 1960 other roadside hamburger stands developed themes, although none duplicated the success of McDonald's franchising. Burger Chef, Burger Queen, Burger Jet, all tried their luck as chains, in addition to Wendy's, Burger King, and ice cream stores, such as Dairy Queen. On the East Coast a diner called the Red Apple Rest, located on a well-traveled route of vacationers leaving New York City for the upstate Catskill Mountains, expanded into a thematic built environment. For a time, it was the most popular stopover point on the family trip between mountains and the city. In the Midwest and parts of the South, the Stuckey Corporation opened franchised strings of roadside restaurants that offered pecan products, sugary confections, and the usual fare of hamburgers and fries to weary automobile passengers. Other examples of multipurpose roadside restaurants, such as the Hadley Farms truckstop outside of Palm Springs, California, abound throughout the motorized American landscape. Many gas stations have also become "one stop" convenience stores servicing transportation with light shopping needs in a new version of the local roadside stand.

As Venturi, Brown and Izenour (1972), observed, the diner is essentially a simple shed adorned with symbols. The *decorated shed* became the forerunner for the themed restaurants of today. Competition among fast-food franchises or restaurants, coupled with increasing affluence and the new consumer norms that support frequent meals outside the home, have pushed eating establishments into competition through the use of thematic devices. Some restaurant chains utilize totally themed environments. Typical of the new trend are the dining places constructed by the Specialty Restaurant Corporation (Wright and Hutchison 1996). They often renovate failed factories. The Cannery in Newport Beach, California, processed sea food from 1921 to 1966, when pollution from suburbanization forced its closure. The interior of the factory was gutted and converted into the Cannery Restaurant. Instead of throwing out the original machinery, however, the designers

Chi-Chi's restaurant, Buffalo, New York, an example of the simulated adobe-style hacienda that signifies Mexican food. Photo by the author.

Hooters restaurant and highway sign. Photo by the author.

recycled it as sculpture. Artifacts from the manufacturing process became part of the decor. Thematic elements, including photographs, ship's compasses, and navigational equipment, were pinned to the walls. Employees dress in uniforms that recall a version of the 1920s. The elements of the cannery motif, therefore, pervade the entire space as a totally themed environment. Of course, the current cannery is only a simulation—not a real fish processing plant, but a fish restaurant disguised as a factory.

Most themed restaurants are synonymous with the image of their franchise chain. The symbolic concordance of a McDonald's carries the exterior theme into its interior. The Cannery looks like a factory on the outside, and continues that theme throughout the interior. The use of themed environmental design, however, is so common today that even places with limited exterior signification often resort to fully themed decor for their interiors. I found one example of this phenomenon while searching for a place to eat in a suburban area outside Pittsburgh, Pennsylvania. I had been staying on a motel row between the city and the regional airport and was dissatisfied with the food prepared by the local motel restaurants. On a quick drive to locate a more promising place to eat, I saw a sign from the highway advertising the "Hacienda" restaurant inside a typical motel. I tried it less out of hunger than of curiosity at finding an anachronistic Mexican eatery on the motel row outside of Pittsburgh.

The place was fully themed in a mass cultural version of Tex-Mex design. Earth-tone painted walls, Aztec printing on the menu, sombreros, cacti, painted chairs and tables, and hot sauce on the counter combined to create that ambience of simulated southwest America familiar from restaurants in Arizona, New Mexico, and places west. After ordering a lunch of typical Mexican fare, I was pleasantly surprised to find that the food was as good as in any other franchised restaurant of that kind in the Southwest. The suburban Pittsburgh "Hacienda" had delivered from simulation to reality with a decent hot meal of burritos, beans and salsa. Furthermore, since I was from southern California at that time, I also enjoyed a reminder of home and was entertained by the simulated space. Themed environments have the capacity of providing enjoyment for their own sake beyond the attractions they contain.

Perhaps the best-known fully themed franchise is the Hard Rock Cafe, which was launched in England. Catering to young adults and serving comparatively simple meals centering on the staple of hamburgers and french fries, this restaurant chain has become so successful that it can be found in the capital cities of several countries. A Hard Rock Casino has recently opened in Las Vegas. The thematic motif of this franchise derives from the rock music industry, including nostalgic elements from its origins in the 1950s. Two signature logos comprise the decor. The exterior of the restaurant is framed by a large guitar outlined in neon. Part of a 1950s Cadillac convertible is embedded in one interior wall where it is easily seen by pa-

trons in all corners of the restaurant. The walls are decorated with both fac-
similes and original memorabilia of the rock industry, including gold
records, concert posters, tour jackets, photographs, and the guitars of famous singers encased in special displays. Waiters and waitresses wear standard restaurant uniforms and the menu is virtually the same whether you
dine at the Cafe in London, Los Angeles, or Tel Aviv. The distinctive motif,
fed constantly by the connection to the rock industry, is developed further
by ambitious merchandising made available at all restaurant locations, including sales of Hard Rock Cafe T-shirts with the location on the logo, jackets and Hard Rock Cafe tote bags.

Because the totally themed environment proved successful for the Hard
Rock Cafe franchise, its form has been copied more recently by other operations. Perhaps the most spectacular example is the chain called Planet Hollywood started by several movie superstars—Arnold Schwarzenegger,
Sylvester Stallone and Bruce Willis, among others. As with the Hard Rock
Cafe, Planet Hollywood commodifies its connection to a popular culture industry—movies. Its walls are decorated with Hollywood memorabilia.
Once inside a typical franchise, the customer can order virtually the same
type of fare as at the Hard Rock Cafe—basic American diner food. Other
than the themed environments of these two examples, there is little to differentiate them from any other local American diner in nearly every town in
the United States.

The *themed* environment makes the difference. Judging from the examples of the Hard Rock Cafe, linked to the rock industry, and Planet Hollywood, linked to the movie industry, popular culture themes can be successfully incorporated by mundane consumption-stimulating environments.
Now there is even a new chain based on the fashion industry and started by
several superstar models. In all these cases, the ordinary but always highly
functional American diner has been transformed through a successful popular culture theme—rock, film, or fashion—into a successful international
restaurant franchise.

Other restaurant franchises that have been less successful feature French
village motifs, southwestern decor, and New York City deli style. A diverse
development of nostalgia themes include 1950s "oldies," farm houses, and
mechanically replicated ethnic symbols such as the quasi-Italian "Olive
Garden" restaurants (more successful than most). A typical nostalgia-
themed restaurant is the "Ruby Tuesday" chain. I find it particularly interesting for its postmodern *implosion* of times and places that stretch over almost an entire century while the decor manages to integrate the varied
referents in the exploitation of popular nostalgia. Its walls are lined with re-
productions of ads and public signs from the 1920s, 1930s, and 1940s. The
decor of the booths, however, reaches further back to the last century. The
booths are illuminated by a remarkable display of imitation Tiffany lamps
(originally dating to the 1890s) and stained glass windows. The nineteenth

and early twentieth century implosion is complemented by "old tyme" ceiling fans and Victorian-era style of hanging plants. Lastly, no Ruby Tuesday's Restaurant would be complete without its authentic looking, but simulated plastic tin roof.

Along with these more dramatically themed environments, famous franchises such as McDonald's, Kentucky Fried Chicken, and Burger King stylize and abstract their identifying logos into equally pervasive motifs that add to the array of signs and symbols within the built environment. One case of abstraction, for example, is the recent alteration of the Kentucky Fried Chicken logo to the stylized letters "KFC" that the company reproduces as part of the decor and as a logo in packaging. More comprehensive examples can be found in the mass production of virtually identical interiors by the McDonald's Corporation. McDonald's capitalizes on the many thematic elements it has produced in advertising over the years, such as the cartoon characters associated with Ronald McDonald and his friends (Ritzer 1993). These signs and McDonald's interior are found around the globe. Anyone familiar with the local hometown McDonald's can successfully negotiate those in Rio de Janeiro, Brazil, Paris, France, Tokyo, Japan, and London, England. Because franchises like Kentucky Fried Chicken and McDonald's are so famous in their own right, promotional advertising develops their names as a corporate theme that functions along with the efficiently designed fast-food interior scheme as a total environment.

The marketing of a restaurant as a thematic environment also deploys aspects of merchandizing to attract customers. Fast-food places often run promotions by providing special gifts that reflect corporate motifs or representative characters. Even when not engaging in special promotions, themed restaurants carry through their coordinated designs down to their napkins, plates, cups, and table decor. As we have seen for the Hard Rock Cafe, they may also extend merchandising to clothing such as T-shirts and jackets that can be a lucrative business in their own right. In addition, stores play matching themed Muzak in the background. There is a close relation between the commercialization of our material environment and the development of commercialized musical environments within work and leisure interiors in our society (Lanza 1993).

Ordinary eateries will liven up menus, like illuminated medieval manuscripts, by designs that represent restaurant symbols or logos. Diners that lack exploited advertising symbols, often bring their decor into concordance with the type of food they serve. Restaurants owned by ethnics—Greeks or Italians for example—include dishes from those cultures along with the standard American fare and commonly have ethnic signs mixed in with generic decorations on tables and menus. A prevalent example of this more subtle theming is the paper hot-cup for take-out coffee (embellished with Greek designs printed in the Greek national colors) used by diners around the country.

The Themed Mall

Malls, just like the restaurants I have discussed, vary regarding the extent to which they carry through thematic designs. Yet, they, too, increasingly use overarching motifs and coordinated design schemes in total environments. As we have seen, restaurants compete with each other for cash customers. Malls began, however, in competition not with other malls, because only recently have they proliferated, but with the downtowns of cities. Their direct competition was for many years the large department stores located in the center of the metropolis. Consequently, they had to advertise themselves as a *place* to go, and they still do. This kind of advertising for a particular space or location within an urban region is, besides the ads placed by individual department stores, aimed at attracting customers to a specific retailing center. As a particular destination, malls require some overarching means of identification. Consequently, as a whole, they often adopt an image meant to be attractive to potential consumers who always have the choice of where to do their shopping. In this way they are different than the city downtown, which is not a unified commercial space and does not advertise itself as a location.

There is another reason malls adopt a unified image. The central city remains a public space that allows free interaction among a variety of people for any number of purposes. The mall is a highly regulated, *private* commercial space that is expressly designed to make money. This instrumental function of the mall, for realizing capital, must be disguised because it would not be attractive to consumers. As a result, almost every mall has an overarching motif that attempts to convey it as a unique and desirable location for its own sake. As with restaurants, the mall theme is a simulation, a facade, but as a motif for the entire space it sets the symbolic tone for the interior.

There are several motifs commonly adopted by malls around the country. One type, called "ye old kitsch," is exemplified by the Olde Towne Mall in Orange County, California. The interior space contains a pedestrian path lined with artificial gas lamps and park benches. Each store confronts the customer in an image of some old-style emporium of the past. There is even a sign, "police," using nineteenth-century graphics for the mall security office. This kind of conformity between overarching mall motif and the particular facades of interior stores is characteristic of the totally themed environment. The latter is rarer among restaurants, as we have seen, and is more commonly characteristic of malls because of the importance of advertising them as a particular place in competition with other locations. Franchise competition is different, because individual stores are not in competition as locations.

Another frequent motif is called "high tech urban" (Gottdiener 1986). Malls of this type are several stories high. They have skylighted ceilings that recall the parisian arcades once studied by Walter Benjamin (1969; Frisby 1985). They strive for a clean, modern look that accentuates chrome, large plate-glass windows, and flashy neon writing. Perhaps the most famous high tech mall is the Galleria in Milan, Italy. It became so popular as a means of marketing commodities that many mall developers in other countries copied its form. The United States alone has many malls called "The Galleria"—one in Houston, Texas, one in Buffalo, New York, one in Glendale, California, and so on. The original galleria, however, is the Palazzo Vecchio in Florence, Italy, which was constructed during the middle ages. The original galleria is a two-story building with a large interior space without a roof and with the second story open to the interior space. Galleria malls in the United States are all enclosed spaces and may have more than two stories.

Malls have been very effective as commercial spaces. They account for over half of all retailing sales in the United States. In many metropolitan areas, competition from malls has been so severe that they have forced downtown shopping districts out of existence. Buffalo, New York, for example, has several large suburban malls ringing the central city, but the last large department store located downtown closed in 1995. During the 1960s, suburbanization and mall development were so devastating to central cities that they required large infusions of cash from federal government renewal programs to float schemes that would bring customers back downtown. Few of these efforts were successful.

Despite their commercial accomplishments, malls are now locked in fierce competition with each other, because their customers can commute to a variety of alternatives. As a result, owners have resorted to thematic appeals in both the outer design of the mall and its advertising to attract business. Typical of this process is the Galleria, in Riverside, California, a medium-sized city 50 miles east of Los Angeles. Riverside had a one-story mall, built in 1970, that serviced the local area. As the community gained more affluent residents over the next few decades, the mall could not compete with more fashionable "upscale" places in Orange County such as the large South Coast Plaza less than one hour away. In 1990 a consortium of developers invested $100 million to transform the Riverside Mall into "The Galleria." The new mall is two stories high, contains over 120 stores, including four large, "anchoring" department stores, has a cinema and a dual-level parking structure able to accommodate almost 10,000 cars. These specifications are typical of the large suburban shopping mall.

The most important aspect of the new Riverside Galleria was the advertising campaign for the mall itself as a competitive location. This campaign used thematic elements in its core appeal to customers that had once forsaken local shopping for the flashier sites of Orange County. According to the local paper,

Riverside's regional mall reopens tomorrow with a new theme, new promise and new stores. . . . The lofty marketing theme for the grand re-opening of the

Galleria is "Reaching New Heights." But the subliminal message could easily be "Reaching New Customers.". . . The Galleria Gurus are confident that their dolled-up, classed up, two-storied showcase will lure Riverside County shoppers who had defected to the hallowed malls of Orange County (Lucas 1991:1).

Besides creating pressure on cities by competitive retailing locations, malls often use symbolic design devices that expressly recall the central city through simulations. That is, malls have always competed with the urban downtown, but recently suburban malls attempt to replicate these downtowns in design motifs re-creating a simulated "urban" environment. First, they have destroyed the inner city's monopoly on retailing, then they proceeded to co-opt the very image of urban life for mall themes. According to one of the leading southern California architects of malls,

> In essence, the difference between what malls are trying to look like now versus what they were trying to do 10 years ago is that now they're trying to create more of a street scene with a variety of store fronts and architecture. . . . And they're also trying to create an interplay of store merchandise from store to store—which is like a department store with different kinds of merchandise in each section, only now you would consider the whole mall as a large department store and each store is one of those separate departments. . . behind this kind of mall design is the idea of going back to the old sense of community, where there used to be the general store where everyone met and knew each other's name (Knaff 1991:4).

In at least one case, fierce competition has produced a mall that advertises itself as an "anti-mall." This Orange County, California, shopping area, also known as The Lab, caters to young adults who find no use for typical mall stores such as Waldenbooks or The Nature Company, and features retailers known for their alternative clothing or accessory styles. In addition, while many malls around the country discourage teenage loitering, this anti-mall welcomes it and offers places to hang out. Other mall owners are also aware of segmented marketing (discussed above). They aim for a mix of stores among their tenants that appeal to different class and status groups.

As the above discussion implies, suburban malls introduced the dimension of spatial location to retailing competition. In the past, when central city department stores dominated all commerce, only individual stores had to advertise. Once suburbanization reached a mass level, after World War II, and malls were introduced as retailing outlets dispersed within the larger metropolitan region, the downtown of the city became only one location among several alternate destinations for shoppers. Each retailing center, suburban or urban, had to compete with every other center as a possible shopping location of commuters. Besides advertising that expresses competition among stores, therefore, mall advertising also expresses competition among the alternate locations of retailing centers. The latter kind of promotion takes the form of thematic appeals, especially for malls that project a special image of their own. Lately, even central cities have begun to advertise themselves to shoppers. Thus, competition leads to a greater use of themes, and the success of certain malls leads to a preferred form that is a self-contained, total environment like the galleria form. In addition, because of place competition, there is a tendency over time for malls to be bigger and bigger so that more store possibilities are offered to potential visitors.

The largest mall in the United States is the Mall of America in Bloomington, Minnesota, outside the city of Minneapolis. It opened for business August 21, 1992. In many ways, this "megamall" is a separate small city. Developers, therefore, pushed the total environment form of the galleria a step further by constructing a closed but immense interior space (sometimes called a "hyperspace" because of its size, see Jameson 1984). The Mall of America covers 78 acres with over 4 million square feet of floor area that includes 2.5 million of actual retailing space, has over 400 specialty shops and four large department stores, contains a 14-screen movie theater, nightclubs, bars, 9 areas of family entertainment, over 22 restaurants and 23 more fastfood outlets. But that is not all. At the center of this three-story complex, beneath an immense hyperspace of skylights, mall developers located a seven-acre theme park that is run by Knotts Berry Farms of southern California. The park has trees and bushes, a controlled climate, 23 amusement rides including a roller coaster, 14 places to eat, and high tech virtual reality simulations.

Promotion literature for the megamall says that it is as big as 88 football fields, can contain 20 of Rome's St. Peter's Basilicas and is five times as large as the famous Red Square in Moscow. According to its Canadian developers, the megamall site in Minnesota was chosen among alternatives in several states because of key factors, including the presence of 27 million people in the surrounding region, and their above average household income. In addition, local governments put up over $100 million in transportation upgrades for the surrounding area, including the construction of large multistoried parking ramps.

The Mall of America cleverly ties its overarching theme to the grand symbol "America." Developers made up the exterior facade in stars and stripes of red, white and blue. Its patriotic decor can mean so many things to so many different people that it serves as a consummate mass marketing device. Ironically, the original developers of the mall were Middle-Eastern immigrants to Canada, but that did not prevent them from feeding an "all American" simulation to the hungry consumers of the Minneapolis–St. Paul region. The interior of the megamall articulates the polysemic patriotic theme with others shaping the major shopping sections. Restaurants are often like the ones analyzed in the last section with individual themes of their own. Most of them are chain franchises such as Hooters (featuring skimpily clad

Mall of America floor plan.

waitresses), Tony Roma's (a chain of rib restaurants), Ruby Tuesday's, Fat Tuesday, the Alamo Grill (Southwest food), the California Cafe (a simulation of southern California style), and Gators (another diner food chain), among others. Each of these themes relates to each other only in the loosest possible sense as belonging to the tapestry of American folklore simulations.

Retailing activities within the mall subdivides space into four main areas. Each, however, returns to the old standby simulation—a recapturing of urban ambience in a varied version of the city street scene. It seems, so far, that malls cannot escape from their main competitor—the downtown, truly public space of the classic central city. The four shopping areas of the Mall of America are: North Garden: Main Street USA; West Market; South Avenue; East Broadway. The mall's inaugural brochure describes the North Garden area as follows: "This lushly landscaped, serpentine walk extends from the venerable Sears to the eagerly waited Nordstrom. With plant-covered balconies, wooden trellises, gazebos, bridges, and airy skylights, North Garden is Main Street, USA" (Mall of America 1992, p.10). Why North Garden is like a typical main street of this country is not at all clear from the above description, but the Mall promoters make that connection anyway.

The Mall of America; a three-story view. Photo by the author.

The second area, West Market, is a simulated representation of a European style marketplace: "From Nordstrom to Macy's, West Market bustles like an old-fashioned European marketplace. You'll make your way past a variety of carts, street venders, shops and eateries to the fancifully painted shop fronts" (p.11). The urban metaphor continues as the brochure describes the third area, South Avenue. "This upscale promenade between Macy's and Bloomingdale's just might become the Rodeo Drive of the Twin Cities," reads the brochure. "Its sophisticated storefronts recall the great shopping streets of Europe" (p. 12). This description has reached the realm of mixed references and geographical confusion. First compared to Rodeo Drive in

The Mall of America; Camp Snoopy at the center. Photo by the author.

Beverly Hills, California, South Avenue (named for its directional location in the mall) is then described as recalling streets of Europe.

It is possible to ask whether South Avenue is that distinct from West Market and whether the entire mall description as recalling or representing a type of place merely exists as advertising discourse with no real basis in reality. This supercesssion of reality is typical of other themed environments that are also mere simulations of distinct cultural places. The simulated environment is simply a cartoonish facade produced to disguise an ordinary retailing establishment. Aside from the skillful deployment of images it has no relation to any real places or cultures around the globe.

The Mall of America; the food court—also typical of other large malls. Photo by the author.

Finally, the last area of the Mall is known as East Broadway. "From Bloomingdale's to Sears, this upbeat district features sleek storefronts, bright lights and the latest looks from the hottest shops" (p.15). At last, we have escaped the European street. However, we find ourselves in an area just as amorphous and as hard to pin down with any degree of uniqueness. It is clear that the ambience of the Mall of America is produced less by careful re-creation of urban street scenes from this country and Europe, than general designs meant to fit in with the style of stores located in each of the four sections. Thus, the two large department stores, Sears and Nordstrom, dominate North Garden. West Market contains several small shops and places to eat besides the department stores. South Avenue is denoted as the "upscale" section of the Mall with the most expensive stores, while East Broadway possesses shops specializing in glitter, current fashions and more youthful clothes.

Despite its sometimes overreaching metaphors that try to connect with urban spaces in real cities, this mall's decor is only a thinly veiled disguise for what is an immense indoor commercial shopping area. This is true of other malls, too. The grand themed environment of the mall functions as a sign-vehicle that aids its role as a container of many commercial enterprises because it is also attractive as a desirable destination. What makes the Mall of America different are its large scale and overabundance of family entertainment

The Mall of America: The self-regulation of crowds within the central mall space. Photo by the author.

opportunities, including the 7-acre theme park. It represents a consummate linkage between retailing and the effort to attract and entertain families in competition with the downtown of the city, which has little family entertainment. This mall is a totally themed environment, but its motifs, like other malls, are subservient to the principal need of conformity with the decor of its tenant shops. Commercialism and not the overarching themes of the classical city—religion, cosmology, or politics—dominates the contemporary mall form.

Finally, the mall form with its themed restaurants and retailers had been imported onto university campuses. A recent report notes the following:

They stood eye to eye and nose to nose for almost 40 minutes, exchanging heavy talk, soulful looks and angry glares outside Mrs. Field's Cookies at the food court entrance. . . . It was the kind of minor mall world melodrama that plays out all the time whenever kids gather over their Whoppers, Pizza Hut personal pan pizzas, and Freshen's Premium Yogurt—everywhere from Tysons Corner Center in suburban Washington to the Galleria in Dallas and Phipps Plaza in Atlanta. The only difference was that this was no shopping center, it was the student union at Boston University (Applebome 1995:16).

The report goes on to contrast this scene with the one at Harvard University across the Charles River. There, students prefer the elite facilities of elegant dining areas, such as Dunster Hall. "No one expects a Jack in the Box or a Taco Bell in Harvard Yard, though even Harvard will offer an upscale grazing emporium on campus this fall that includes a familiar name or two" (Applebome 1995:16–17).

According to those interviewed, campus administrations find the mall form a promising way of raising revenues. The University of South Carolina, for example, constructed a 14-store shopping center for its students and faculty over 10 years ago. Recently, other campuses also see the virtues of blending a university environment with the commercial attractiveness of the mall. As this report argues, "Increasingly, the culture and values of the mall are coloring the culture and values of the university. . . . Let's face it, Main Street America doesn't exist anymore. Mall America exists. Why should collegiate life be the last bastion of something that doesn't exist anymore?" (Applebome 1995:17) As elsewhere, franchising of food and retailing takes over commerce because of the success of the mall form—the enclosed, themed space of quasi-public communion.

Airports as Themed Environments

Restaurants and malls are themed environments that are familiar as everyday places to visit. More graphic examples of what I have been calling a total themed environment are experienced more on special occasions, such as a journey, a vacation, or an entertainment break. Their calculated design uses an overarching theme and carries it forward through concordant signs within the interior of the built space. One example is the large metropolitan airport.

When commercial air travel was first introduced in the 1920s it incorporated the romance of flying. Of course, airplanes had to compete with the more popular modes of transportation at the time, especially the railroad. Early air carriers stressed the special treatment of passengers by stew-

The terminal building at Dulles International Airport. Note the symbolic architecture suggesting flight. Photo courtesy of UPI/Bettmann.

ardesses, the availability of in-flight meals, and comfortable seats. Then, airports were rather humdrum affairs. After World War II, when air travel had become a generally accepted mode of long distance transportation, the design of air terminals became an important part of the transportation industry. Air travel had always been relatively expensive, but by 1960 declining fares due to price wars combined with a burgeoning consumer demand from the growing middle class to produce a *mass market* for commercial air transportation. Airport authorities and commercial carriers turned increasingly to the use of themes in promoting their respective services, and they resurrected the glamour of flight.

In the United States, unlike other industrialized countries, it is the local municipal authorities that build and run airports. However, their terminals are the property of individual airlines. The latter can do little to affect the decor of the entire complex, but they do have control over their own service space. Few airports have been built since World War II, but there have been many terminal renovations. The most impressive new airport constructions were Kennedy International in the 1950s, Dulles Airfield in the 1960s, the Dallas–Ft. Worth complex in 1974, and, after a twenty-year hiatus, the Denver International airport that opened in 1995. Terminal renovations, in contrast, have occurred frequently and in response to advertising needs and competition from other airlines. In addition, airport terminals are rejuvenated in response to the needs of local authorities for more revenue. Lately, both terminal and airport renovations have increasingly resorted to themed environments in their efforts to improve their competitive positions or to adjust to new technologies of flight.

For example, in the 1970s the major carriers introduced wide-bodied jets. Until then airports had handled smaller planes. The new jets required more room and terminals across the country had to be renovated to handle the new space demands. At that time O'Hare airport, outside Chicago, was the busiest in the nation. Authorities altered their facilities to handle the larger planes that required an expansion of the embarking-disembarking space, or the *concourse* area. As with other airports around the country, expansion necessitated the construction of new concourse spaces linked to the old central terminal. Each airline had to renovate concourse spaces by itself, because each was responsible for its own terminal. United Airlines launched an ambitious redevelopment scheme that included the construction of two concourses, B and C, within the airport terminal area. They were separated, unfortunately, by the expanse of the airport runway. United constructed an underground tunnel that connected the two concourses and solved this dilemma. The airline's problems, however, were only beginning. The main issue facing the airline was not only how to construct the underground connection, but how to design the linking space to attract customers who would overlook the inconvenience of the relatively long trek between the concourses.

At an early stage in facing this marketing problem, the airline invited the Walt Disney Corporation to help design a user-friendly tunnel space that included diorama displays along its walls (Bruegmann 1989:8). Performing what seems like a reflex action at the time, the airline sought immediately to solve its problem by using a themed environment produced by the acknowledged master of theme parks. The original architect of the terminal renovation, Helmut Jahn, however, objected on aesthetic grounds. He convinced United to commission an undulating light and music sculpture which was more abstract in design and would fill the volume of tunnel space. The foundation for the proposed work of art used an organic theme of growth and continuity. As one architecture historian notes, "In the [proposed] model, undulating walls of glass flowed with light reflected from a colored wall behind. . . . The glowing glass wall continued to flow up into the ceiling in a structure resembling the trunk and branches of trees, and the space was capped by a series of brilliantly colored tubes running the length of the tunnel" (Bruegmann 1989:8).

After construction, many travelers strongly criticized the tunnel environment. They objected, in particular, to the type of computerized music played along its length. The effect of the lights and music was quite startling to passengers who had come to expect unobtrusive decors in their travels. For a while the underground design was a controversial topic in local newspapers and also in United's business meetings. Eventually, United changed the music and adjusted the light sculpture to more average tastes, but not before a good deal of negotiations and controversy (Bruegmann 1989).

As this case shows, themed environments are not always embraced by consumers. Despite their growing popularity as a marketing solution, they can be problematical to customers. Airports in particular seem to have their share of problems with the design of renovations, perhaps because they are combined private and public facilities that can mix the worst of both worlds—local municipal politics and corporate wrangling over marketing schemes.

To take another and more recent example, in the 1990s the city of Denver abandoned its municipal airport and built a larger one 23 miles east of the city at a cost of $3.2 billion. The new Denver International Airport was plagued with many construction and political problems before its opening in 1995. It also has its share of signification problems. A great deal of money was invested in the unusual Jeppesen Terminal Building that was constructed of 34 spires and a white, tensile fabric roof. It is difficult to say what it is meant to symbolize. Consequently, the airport authority has had to work overtime to define the meaning of the design. According to brochures available at the airport, "The white peaks of the Jeppesen Terminal, visible from several miles, are reminiscent of the Rocky Mountains." This grand architectural scheme has received mixed reviews. As in the O'Hare tunnel case, perhaps the story of the Denver design awaits a new round of negotiations regarding its symbolic content.

In many ways the large open spaces of contemporary airline terminals are reminiscent of the massive interior spaces produced by mall construction. Furthermore, as traffic has expanded to millions each day, it is not surprising that the two functions—air transfer and retailing, or the air terminal and the mall—merged through conscious design. Actually, airports have served as retailing sites for some time. International travelers, in particular, can obtain commodities without paying import taxes provided they purchase them in "duty-free" shops. After World War II, when propeller-driven planes were still standard, several airports around the globe, such as at Shannon, Ireland, nurtured duty-free shopping. As flight equipment and transfer patterns changed, different airports became hubs for passenger traffic and also capitalized on duty free shopping. Due to the ease with which people can cross borders in Western Europe, some of the best developed airport shopping areas arose in terminals on the continent. The bustling nodal points of Frankfurt International in Germany and the Zurich airport in Switzerland are two examples of airports that have extensive concourse space devoted to duty-free shopping. These retailing outlets resemble large American supermarkets and come equipped with shopping carts and laser-scanning check out registers.

A view of the new Jeppesen terminal at Denver International airport silhouetting the ambiguously symbolic design. Photo courtesy of The Bettmann Archive.

Always the basic design of airport retailing relies on the broad expanses created by concourse-oriented terminal development. With extensive pathways to and from planes, passengers can also be viewed as consumers with some time on their hands. Shops hoping to capitalize on the need for diversion advertise their wares along the broad concourses. This array resembles in form the fully enclosed shopping mall.

Within the confines of the United States, airport retailing was a neglected activity. Even when extensive concourse renovation began, such as in the United facility at O'Hare, the sidelines were dedicated to rather unimaginative, utilitarian shops selling newspapers, limited snacks, alcohol, local knick-knacks, or traveler aids, such as luggage or drugs. During the late 1980s, however, several airports began to take the lesson of duty-free retailing to heart and expanded their commercial functions within renovated concourse spaces. One of the most expansive projects was the transformation of the Pittsburgh airport into an airport-shopping mall, acknowledged now as "the leader in airport retail operations" (Johnson 1995:F–2). Officials invited upscale retailers common to suburban malls to open stores within the terminal structure and many did. This airport contains 80 restaurants and retail shops.

Most air travelers have experienced considerably higher prices for food and commodities at airports than at shopping malls. But at the Pittsburgh airport, retailers have agreed to keep their prices at the same level as at the malls. This practice, new to airport retailing, is known as "guaranteed street pricing." Therefore, the airport acts like a mall and attracts local shoppers who have no immediate interest in air transportation. Sales have been impressive and in 1994 averaged almost seven dollars for every boarded passenger (Johnson 1995).

Pittsburgh's success has inspired other airports to become shopping meccas. LaGuardia Airport in New York City, for example, recently completed a renovation of its main terminal and concourse areas that includes an extensive shopping space. Here, as elsewhere, the mall form is followed because it fits so well the shape of the terminal concourse.

Finally, the new Denver International Airport boasts many shops and mall-type retailing outlets. In this case, it was designed from the beginning as a combined airport and mall, rather than as an innovation following extensive renovation. Each of the three concourses has several levels that offer considerable consumption alternatives. Concourse A, for example, has four restaurant-delis, snack shops, apparel stores, a children's museum, and banking services. Concourse B has seven restaurants, a fast-food court, more specialty apparel stores, gift shops (including the franchise chains The Nature Company and The Body Shop), and a chiropractor's office. Concourse C contains four restaurants, five apparel-gift shops, a bank and an "airport family fun center." Other similar shops are in the main terminal building. Unlike the Pittsburgh airport that is easily accessible from the city, however, the Denver facilities are aimed directly at the large volume of passenger traffic anxiously anticipated in the future, because the site is so far from the population center of the city.

The expansive concourse spaces created by the new air terminals are not exploited only by retailers. In Nevada, where gambling is legal, airports are mere extensions of casino spaces. The McCarran Airfield in Las Vegas, for example, has slot machines in every available place throughout the concourse area. It is possible to engage in traditional casino games, including blackjack (on automated machines) and slots, without leaving the terminal.

Airport cuisine, once restricted to the most basic forms of food and drink, now provides an impressive array of choices as aspects of the mall food court are adopted by terminals. Eating facilities are located along the new concourse renovations, and many of these are franchises from fast food chains familiar to mall shoppers. Terminals and concourses, such as at O'Hare, also have food courts and restaurant clusters that are home to several kinds of commercial eateries, including varied ethnic foods: Mexican, Chinese, Italian, and delicatessen. An extensive dining selection is planned for the renovated Los Angeles Airport, including major chains such as Kentucky Fried Chicken and smaller but well-known franchises, such as Wolfgang Puck and the Panda Express.

Increasingly, then, the mall and the airport merge in design. With this conjuncture, the same thematic dynamics discussed in the case of malls also applies to the new retailing places in air terminals. These enclosed, themed spaces capture the pedestrian mode of urban street culture for the purposes of commerce, even in places such as airports whose primary function is something else.

In short, airports are interesting themed environments not because they overwhelm us with highly coordinated themes, as with restaurants such as the Hard Rock Cafe, but because they are overendowed with sign systems. Airports are extreme cases of semantized environments. They require functional sign systems to guide people to and from planes and local streets. As transport hubs they facilitate multidimensional traffic movement with easy to decipher, graphically *denotative* sign systems. But there is a second dimension to their symbols. Within the airport interior, signification processes have altered with the architectural shift from an emphasis on waiting room and ticketing spaces, the old railroad metaphor, to airy, well-lit pedestrian concourses that facilitate the changing of flights. These spaces are overlaid with sign systems deriving from consumer retailing and mass marketing. Here the airport space has been transformed into a type of shopping mall. As such, the interior built environment intersects with the consumer culture propagated in mass media advertising and commercial marketing with its cornucopia of signs and sign systems.

CHAPTER FIVE

The Las Vegas Casino, the Theme Park, and the Further Extension of Themed Environments

Restaurants, malls, and airports are environments that people use every day to carry out their tasks of living and working. They have experienced increased competition for customers because of alternate locations that are now easy to reach. Retailing and restaurants, in particular, are no longer dependent on the central city, ethnic neighborhoods, or business districts. They can be found throughout the ever-expanding metropolitan region and draw for their customers on the ability of people to commute to and from preferred consumer locations, work, and home. As we have seen, with competition has also come an increasing reliance on the use of themed environments. By using architectural and retailing elements that appeal to shoppers, built forms like the mall have achieved a commercial success rivaling that of central business districts. The mall is not just a location for buying commodities, however. It is very much a *place*, an important space, just like the downtown central city area that draws people to it for a variety of reasons.

Another kind of themed environment, however, departs from the everyday. Within this group are examples that function as desirable spaces in their own right, so much so that they are specific destinations for people on vacation. Mall-type places are designed as commercial, merchandising areas first, but they are also entertainment spaces. The places considered in this section reverse that structure. They are constructed principally as ludic centers or entertainment spaces, with merchandising as a secondary function. Because they are meant to entertain, their commercial value becomes the space itself and they may charge admission. Let us examine these special places.

Las Vegas Casinos

Almost a quarter century ago, three architects, Robert Venturi, Denise S. Brown, and Steven Izenour, published a spectacularly prescient book, *Learning from Las Vegas* (1972). In their exhaustive study of the Las Vegas architecture of that time they identified a new design phenomenon, namely, the rejection of modernist architecture that ignores symbols in favor of buildings that emphasized signs and symbols of all kinds. According to the authors, and as I have discussed in Chapter 2, modernist architecture sought to escape from the use of symbols and adopted instead an austere program of design that stressed blank walls of glass, steel, and simple rectangles like most tall skyscrapers found in central cities today. According to modernist architectural theory, structures expressed meaning through the characteristics of form rather than through symbol and allusion. Buildings were sign-vehicles of their social function. As Venturi and his associates observed during their visits to Las Vegas in the late 1960s and early 1970s, however, its architecture represented a thorough rejection of modernism. It was built as if modernist doctrines never existed.

The Las Vegas casino environment is a multidimensional system of signs. Both the built forms and the messages they intend to convey are highly developed and articulated as intentional symbols. Signs exist everywhere. They direct traffic off the main interstate highway to the streets on which the various hotel-casinos can be found. They advertise individual casinos and their attractions, such as food and headliner entertainment. The signs also amuse through computer generated electronic light displays. Unlike the "hyposignificant" urban spaces produced by modernism, the built environment of Las Vegas is overendowed with signification and meaning. Whereas in our previous discussions I have noted that forms such as malls, restaurants, and airports may vary regarding the extent that they systematically incorporate themes within the built space, Las Vegas is an entire metropolitan area that is quite literally themed.

The symbolic environment fits the needs of an automobile-dominated landscape with immense distances and high-speed travel "where the subtleties of pure architectural space can no longer be savored" (Venturi, Brown, and Izenour, 1972:153). The vast spaces of the desert-dominated Southwest with its fast-paced interstate highways requires a commercial environment with "explicit and heightened symbolism" composed of "watts, animation, and iconology" (p.19). The function of the Las Vegas themed environment is straightforward—the seduction of the consumer. Las Vegas is a multi-dimensional experience of seductive pleasures—money, sex, food, gambling, and nightlife. Las Vegas constitutes a specialized space, it is one of several global "pleasure zones," like Monte Carlo and the French Riviera (the Riviera is also the name of a Las Vegas Casino), the Greek islands, Rio de Janeiro (the name of another Las Vegas casino), Disneyworld, Marienbad, and the Taj Mahal. According to Venturi and associates, "Essential to the imagery of pleasure-zone architecture are lightness, the quality of being an oasis in a hostile context, heightened symbolism, and the ability to engulf the visitor in a new role: vacation from everyday reality" (p.53).

Las Vegas as a whole signifies a contrast from the blandness of southwest suburban environments such as Los Angeles, and the heat of the desert.

Signs in Las Vegas use mixed media—words, pictures, and sculpture—to persuade and inform. A sign is contradictorily, for day and night. The same sign works as polychromic sculpture in the sun and as black silhouette against the sun; at night it is a source of light. It revolves by day and becomes a play of lights at night. It contains scales for close up and distance (p.51). . . . Day is negated inside the casinos and night negated on the Strip. The signs are, contradictorily, for day *and* night (p.77).

Beyond the uniqueness of Las Vegas as a fully themed environment, the individual casinos develop motifs and possess concordant sign systems that express some of the most vivid fantasies of American culture. Advertisements for Las Vegas casino-resorts develop these fantasy themes through signs, sculptures, and three-dimensional light and sound shows that are often incredibly elaborate. Fantasy themes are developed through language and pictures that *connote* a specific ideology or set of cultural meanings relating to the announced theme. The metaphorical relation is declared both as a unifying motif exploited within the interior of the casino and developed as a particular set of connotations by the design of the exterior or facade of the casino-hotel.

For example, Caesar's Palace Hotel and Casino has an exterior designed as an immense Roman villa. This motif is carried forward throughout the interior design elements that always refer to a fantasy version of Rome. Even the cocktail waitresses wear uniforms that recall that style. This environment, therefore, is totally themed by one motif. Near Caesar's is the Mirage Hotel and Casino, another place with a totally themed environment. This highly successful resort develops several motifs. However, the dominant one is "tropical paradise," seemingly a contradiction because its name, Mirage, signifies a desert phenomenon. But, in Las Vegas, no one seems to care. The Mirage develops its themes through both exterior displays and interior design (more later).

This complexity of fantasy motifs and the rapid-fire transmission of distinct messages is communicated to cars passing along the major interstate and the local streets by the literal signs of Las Vegas. The messages simultaneously denote specific information such as the content and price of a meal, and connote thematic associations and invitations to participate in a fantasy environment.

The Las Vegas gambling economy is situated within structures that are combinations of casinos, hotels, and resorts. Most of the spectacular resort-casinos are on the north-south route of Las Vegas Boulevard, also known as "the Strip" because of the need for sprawling space. In contrast, the downtown area, "Glitter Gulch," is dominated by casinos, which specialize in gambling, or hotel-casinos like the Golden Nugget, that exploit the original theme of Las Vegas as a Wild West paradise.

According to Venturi and associates, the casino structures are examples of the "decorated shed." They are simple buildings designed for gambling or hotel occupancy that are overlaid by elaborate signs. Decorated and lit with neon graphics, the Las Vegas casino functions as one big sign. Each casino possesses a separate theme—that is, some overarching code or ideology that reflects some desirable fantasy aspect of American culture. The varied thematic devices, with the casino functioning as one large sign of itself, creates

Las Vegas, the MGM Grand entrance. Photo by the author.

Las Vegas, the sphinx in front of the Luxor Casino and Hotel. Photo by the author.

Las Vegas, the Excalibur Casino and Hotel. Photo by the author.

Las Vegas, Kon Tiki Village in the back lot of the Hotel Tropicana.
Photo by the author.

an emergent system of signification through difference. Each differentiated casino with its separate theme, standing juxtaposed against other casinos, produces an overarching intertextuality that is the grand text of Las Vegas—a system of difference at the level of casinos themselves. This grand text does not intend to convey any particular message, but, instead, becomes the profusion of signs that is the total environmental experience of Las Vegas. As owners alter individual casino themes, or when they build new casinos, the system of difference also changes and the Las Vegas experience becomes more varied and deeply modulated.

Las Vegas street scene: Note the postmodern implosion of symbols from ancient Egypt, the European middle ages, Polynesian stone heads, and cars. Photo by the author.

Starting from the southern tip of Las Vegas Boulevard (the Strip), and working northward, the following casinos and their overarching themes are juxtaposed. The Hacienda Hotel is furthest south and displays a Mexican-Southwest fantasy theme. The visitor going north on the same side of the street is tempted by the spectacular hotels—the Luxor, an Egyptian pyramid fantasy, and the Excalibur, a medieval castle and King Arthur fantasy. The Tropicana casino with its highly articulated, tropical Brazilian-Polynesian fantasy is across the street.

The MGM Grand, the largest casino-hotel in the world, is north of the Tropicana. Its entrance is an illuminated lion. The Grand elaborates the theme of Hollywood glamour and MGM memorabilia. Further north is the Aladdin, with its Arabian Nights theme, and Bally's, which exploits the ambiance of continental luxury and a "Monte Carlo" setting. The Dunes Hotel-Casino once stood across the street from the Aladdin. It also exploited an Arabian theme, but was demolished in 1993 to make way for a larger, more profitable project. It shares the block with several small motel-inns including the Broadway and the La Quinta, that exploit thematic devices in their motel logos, although they lack the elaboration and development of the casinos.

Crossing Flamingo Road on the west side of the Strip we encounter the Caesar's Palace complex, which has undergone several expansions. The Palace modulates the overarching themes of Caesar's Rome and classical Italian architecture. Caesar's also contains a fully enclosed mini-shopping mall at its entrance. The mall's only exit is through the gambling casino. Across the street is the Barbary Coast, with its theme of old-time, nineteenth century San Francisco, and the Flamingo (Bugsy Siegal's hotel) that retains its twin themes of continental luxury and Hollywood glamour. North of the Flamingo is the Imperial Palace that has limited thematic elements associated with Asia or Japan, and the Holiday Inn Motel.

The giant Mirage complex is across the street, on the west side. It exploits both Hollywood glamour and tropical paradise themes. For the benefit of passersby on the Strip, the Mirage has a spectacular display of an erupting volcano, repeated nightly every 15 minutes. The Treasure Island casino-hotel (further north) offers a nightly repeating show outside its building depicting a battle between two ships within an artificial Caribbean lagoon. The scale of this display is spectacular and includes live actors.

Further up the Strip to the borders of downtown and Glitter Gulch, we find the Sands Hotel-Resort-Casino and the Desert Inn—both with an Arabian Nights theme. Across the Strip, the Frontier Hotel, which introduces a Wild West, cowboy theme for the first time and allows a thematic segue into the downtown with its overly endowed Wild West themed casinos such as the Golden Nugget, Binions Horseshoe and the Four Queens. It was precisely this cowboy motif that was exploited as the thematic referent for the old Las Vegas, before the extensive Strip development of recent years abandoned it for spectacular consumer fantasies.

Before entering the downtown area we encounter several other large casinos. The Stardust is on the west side of the Strip, next to the Frontier. It is an immense hotel-motel complex that expresses a limited association with Hollywood glamour. Heading north we find the Westward Ho casino that exploits the downtown cowboy theme. The gigantic Circus Circus complex, with an obvious circus theme, includes a recently completed theme park and has round-the-clock performances of live circus acts. On the east side of the street are several small hotel-casinos and the Riviera Casino-hotel that displays a continental, Monaco–French Riviera theme. North of it is the Wet and Wild water theme park and on the city limits boundary (or Sahara Avenue), we find the Sahara Hotel, another Arabian fantasy thematic attraction.

Taken as a whole, by combining the experience of the Strip and the downtown, the juxtaposition of these casino themes produces a spectacular profusion of signs that defines the Las Vegas environment. Standing at the entrance of the Tropicana Hotel-Casino, for example, one can see in a single scopic gaze a giant Easter Island sculpted head (now removed by new construction), an immense three-story lion (MGM Grand entrance), the medieval edifice of the Excalibur castle, and the giant sandstone Sphinx and slate pyramid of the Luxor. Within the field of view one can also see tall gas station signs with their corporate logos, gigantic casino signs advertising food and showcase entertainment, bus stops, parking lot signs, and advertising for various products on walls and fences.

With new construction and the density of spectacular themed casinos at the southern end of Las Vegas Boulevard has also come escalating density in pedestrian traffic. Las Vegas as a whole has become a theme park. The activity of casino hopping has taken on a new caché and relevance as the built environment produces signification through thematic differences. Pedestrians derive pleasure by walking among the casinos in this symbolic space. They make their way from the spectacular edifices at the southern end of the strip, especially the Luxor and the MGM Grand, and walk several blocks north up to the Mirage–Treasure Island complex with its spectacular exterior light and sound shows that encourage pedestrian activity on the streets.

As Venturi and associates have pointed out, competition in thematic displays always leads to larger and more spectacular signs. This is certainly the case in recent years as casinos have shifted to staged productions, simulations, and other spectacular forms such as theme parks, and immense statues like the sphinx in front of the Luxor and the lion entrance to the MGM Grand. Such intense competition over themes has also produced a new Las Vegas experience centered, not on the exterior play of fantasy differences among casinos, but within the constructed space itself. By catering to the growing market of family visitors, several casinos have built immense theme parks that offer Disney-style rides and attractions. The MGM Grand, Circus Circus, and the Luxor offer self-contained theme parks with sophisticated rides. The desire to stimulate family vacation visitors has resulted in the fashioning of large virtual reality rooms with computerized games for children. The interior of the Luxor pyramid is particularly impressive as it contains a variety of virtual reality attractions that cater to both adults and children and an immense virtual reality video arcade for kids.

A final characteristic of Las Vegas involves the role of thematic elements in the development of the gambling economy. Competition among casinos involves competition through differentiating sign values. As in other cases we have discussed, such as restaurants and malls, Las Vegas casinos compete with each other through signs. Competition for customers pushes reliance on thematic appeals and this, in turn, defines the quality of development for the entire Las Vegas metro region. The area has become one large theme park. Las Vegas is the best example of the proposition argued for by this book that today's style of economic competition increasingly forces commercial enterprises to rely on evermore elaborate thematic appeals.

Competition through signs and image-based differentiation exploits the symbolic value of products, rather than their use or exchange values. As the former type of competition comes to define the economy, we progress toward a postmodern culture where sign value dominates all transactions, as our discussion of Baudrillard suggests (see Chapter 2). In Las Vegas, the commodity sold to consumers—gambling or games of chance—is relatively uniform from casino to casino. One advantage of a visit to Las Vegas is that consumers familiar with games of chance have little difficulty orienting themselves to particular casinos, no matter which one they choose. They can also travel from casino to casino and indulge in gaming with little need to adjust their mind-sets in the gambling frame of activity. There are, however, aficionados who claim that some casinos offer slightly better odds than others and that some differences in product exist. But for the overwhelming majority of Las Vegas customers, these differences are not enough to send them packing from one casino to another.

Due to product uniformity, thematic appeals are the basis of Las Vegas advertising. First, casinos display a unified interest in enticing people to visit Las Vegas as opposed to other alternatives, such as local Indian gaming. This is accomplished by advertising that sells a generalized and desirable Las Vegas image as a proposed vacation location, much the way malls advertise as a desirable destination for shoppers. Television and newspaper ads hype the Las Vegas lifestyle in the hope of stimulating tourism. This popularly constructed style of life, produced by advertising as a simulation, has come to represent Las Vegas in the minds of many people. Second, and most significant, casinos invest in elaborate themes that they hope will differentiate themselves from rivals. These overarching motifs not only define the decor of the exterior and interior but are also exploited as symbols in advertising.

Until the present, Las Vegas themes have drawn from a narrow but increasingly more diverse repertoire of sources. Earliest casino fantasies borrowed from associations with casino gambling around the world, such as the Wild West, Monte Carlo, or Riviera motifs, or an association with Hollywood. More recently, casino designs have plundered the past by resurrecting the themes of medieval Europe, Rome, and ancient Egypt. Other casinos drew more directly from fantasy motifs that never really existed, such as the repeated representations of the Arabian Nights or the "tropical paradise." All these symbolic appeals are quite common to our popular culture. It is interesting to speculate where Las Vegas environments might be going in the future.

From recent accounts of proposed developments it seems that the planned casino-resorts will draw most directly on an urban motif. One proposal, for example, involves a casino re-creation of New York City and another of Paris. New York-New York Hotel and Casino is being developed by the MGM Grand corporation. It will have 2,119 rooms and an exterior designed in the shape of the Manhattan skyline, including a 48-story, 525 foot-high version of the Empire State Building. The Bally Entertainment Corporation announced its plans recently for a 2,500-room mega-resort modeled after Paris that will feature a 50-story reproduction of the Eiffel Tower.

These examples suggest that the urban ambiance and street culture of the large, historically significant central city, rather than depictions of popular fantasies, is the preferred direction of new casino planning. In this sense proposed thematic environments aim to capture both the scale of the city and its unique culture of pedestrian space where chance encounters, specialized commercial shopping, restaurants, and the street milieu of the urban walker intermingle. This is very much like the way malls function as well. Because this type of city culture is increasingly on the decline in the United States within existing urban places, this future trend for Las Vegas casinos is quite ironic. As cities die, they are recycled as images and themes for Las Vegas Casinos. One can say, then, that Las Vegas casinos keep urban culture alive in a certain fashion. The city itself has become a theme park. New York or Paris are replaced by a casino simulating New York or Paris just as Epcot Center in Disneyworld simulates visits to other countries.

As discussed in Chapter 3, this shift to image and simulation has negative as well as positive aspects. It is, perhaps, wrong to lament the simulated superficiality of Las Vegas architecture, as some critics continue to do despite the best efforts of architect-commentators, such as Robert Venturi, and the recent rise of postmodernism. These fantasy facades have always functioned to hide the main purpose of the building—casino gambling. It is the latter that should be examined with more concern as the basis for an urban economy, because casino gambling is now proposed as a general panacea for many depressed places in the United States as its manufacturing strength declines. Beyond the issue of gambling as the basis for the local economy, there is a second concern. Although we can only marvel at the popularity of simulated urban environments in the new Vegas architecture, we may rightly wonder why, at the same time, this society allows its real cities to languish further in decay and decline.

The Theme Park

The most spectacularly successful creation of a special place that is a themed environment is Disneyland in Anaheim, California. Along with the much larger Disneyworld in Orlando, Florida, the Disney theme park form is the most popular attraction on the earth. It has been exported to Japan and France and has influenced both the construction and operation of similar themed amusement parks the world over. Unlike the symbolic forms encountered in daily life, the theme park is a destination that people choose for special recreational breaks—especially family vacations. When most visitors go to Disneyworld, for example, they do so as families who have flown in from another area and have arranged hotel accommodations during the period that they will be visiting the park.

What was so remarkable about the original Disneyland that produced the global mass phenomenon of the popular theme park? We might guess that corporate advertising and the close link between Disneyland and the many films of the Disney Company fueled the popularity and acceptability of the images and fantasies upon which the park experience was based. In addition, as discussed in Chapter 3, theme parks have important antecedents in world expositions and state fairs whose features the present attractions exploit. Surely these factors are a major part of the success story. However, at the time of its construction, in the 1950s, Disneyland provided an encounter for its visitors that was so unique and compelling that it became a new form of commercial enterprise. People not only visited the park for the rides or merchandise that it offered, as they do at state fairs, but also for admission to the park itself. Experience of the themed built environment, for Disneyland, is its own reward, as it is also for the large, fully-enclosed mall and other successful themed environments. The difference between them is that the theme park charges admission to the total space, which is organized around a central motif that is then consumed through the physical actions of the visitors.

Disneyland

By the early 1990s, more than 300 million people had visited Disneyland—many more people than the present population of the United States. Built on a 160-acre former orange grove, the original Disneyland opened in 1955 at a cost of $17 million. Then many critics argued that the park would not succeed because it did not possess the typical amusement rides, such as a Ferris Wheel. But Disney, who went into debt to build the attraction, was not offering a collection of rides. His park was a fantasy environment, and that aspect became one source of Disneyland's success. As an architectural critique observed, "It is an almost faultless organization for delivering, against cash, almost any type at all of environmental experience that human fancy however inflamed, could ever devise. Here are pedestrian piazzas, seas, jungles, castles, outerspace, Main Street, the Old West, mountains, more than can be experienced in a single day's visit" (Banham 1971:127).

The park experience fits into and reinforces the merchandising effort of the Disney Corporation contributing to its success. Walt Disney was one of the first businessmen to create a consumer market exclusively for children through the retailing of toy products based on his movies. Although most people's incomes during the 1930s were relatively low, Disney had already succeeded in merchandising spinoff items, following the success of his cartoons. As one historian has noted about the social significance of Disney's early efforts in the 1930s, "By cross-marketing toys and movies Disney was able to convince critics that movies were not harmful to children, while *persuading children* to gain satisfaction through shopping" (Heller 1994:A9).

Both parents and children enjoyed the Disney creations at the movies. As the scale of merchandising increased, people around the globe became familiar with Disney characters and spinoff products. By the 1980s, when Disneyworld was built in Orlando, Florida, the themed elements of the park's experience were ubiquitously familiar. According to one writer, "Struggle as we may, it's impossible for Americans to discover Disneyland. The first visit feels like a trip back. From whatever angle, nothing looks fake. Fabricated, yes, fake no. Disneyland isn't the mimicry of a thing; it's a thing" (Carson 1992:17).

Over the years Disneyland has attracted its share of criticism (see Sorkin 1992). It is reviled for its crass commercialism, for the very merchandising from films that is the basis of its early success, and for its alleged escapism and simulation (see Baudrillard 1983). One of the most penetrating criticisms is of the consummate skill with which the park planners engineer both crowd control and crowd movement. As Carson observes,

> Militaristic the place isn't; it's hard to be martial in pastel. But militating, certainly. As you queue in those ingenious waiting lines, or stroll in obedience to a traffic flow whose engineering you never register, or take on bric-a-brac at concession areas designed not as breaks in the continuity but proofs of it, what you and your 10 or 20 thousand cohorts are performing is a huge, choreographed, aesthetically quite arresting species of close-order drill in mufti (1992:18).

Disneyland has also attracted the admiration of some important city planners of the country, such as James Rouse, the developer of many commercial themed environments and the new town Columbia, Maryland (Gottdiener 1994:103). According to Charles Moore, "People often use Disneyland as a synonym for the facile, shallow and fake. It just doesn't wash. This incredibly energetic collection of environmental experiences offers enough lessons for a whole architectural education in all the things that matter—community and reality, private memory and inhabitation, as well as some technical lessons in propinquity and choreography" (quoted in Carson 1992:20). Some observers have even remarked about the *utopian* nature of Disney town planning. They note that its physical infrastructure performs remarkably well, especially given the large numbers of people visiting the park daily. Whatever its appeal to architects and designers, we know that, over the years, Disneyland has had a profound impact on the construction of themed environments across the country by blending common mass culture symbols and an appealing physical design. Let us examine this phenomenon more closely, because of its great influence.

The Structure of the Park

The theme park known as Disneyland has a definite structure that is also replicated from Disneyland to Disneyland wherever the global location. The area is fronted by a large parking lot in which visitors must abandon their cars and become pedestrians as their very first act upon arrival. As in the case of the mall or the urban arcade of the 19th century, the themed environment transforms the average pedestrian with her/his multifaceted personality into a consumer for commercial purposes. This shift from multifaceted self to consumer-self is accomplished by a fantasy environment.

At the entrance they purchase tickets that allow them full access to the rides inside. The grand entrance of Disneyland is a simulation of Main Street America and represents Walter Disney's idealization of the small Midwestern town where he grew up. Main Street is a bisecting road that serves as the gateway to the rest of the park and along its sides retailers sell assorted Disney merchandise. Disneyland contains four separate realms, three representations of towns and an open-air center that features food and entertainment. Disneyworld, in Orlando, Florida, is even more elaborate with several adjoining parks, including Epcot Center.

Each realm of the Disneyland environment represents domains developed by the Disney Corporation in films and television shows over the years. They are: Tomorrowland—a sophomoric representation of futurism; Frontierland—the scene of old Disney successes, such as Davey Crockett and a representation of the early days of American settlement; Adventureland—escapist fantasies ranging from Tom Sawyer rafting to safari jungle cruises; and Fantasyland—the virtual site of Disney cartoon fantasies and animated films. Fantasyland contains the mock Matterhorn mountain and Sleeping Beauty's Castle (which could also be Snow White's or Cinderella's); the latter usually serves as the distinguishing feature or sign of Disneyland in publicity images and is at the end of the gateway road that begins at Main Street.

The three mock towns of the park consist of the already mentioned Main Street; New Orleans Square, which is an open air mini-center that features food and is the site of some of the more popular park rides such as Pirates of the Caribbean; and Toontown, which was recently added to the classic form of Disneyland after the success of the film, Roger Rabbit. Amusement rides are distributed all around the park area within each realm and mini-center. The landscape is upgraded from time to time by the addition or subtraction of attractions. For example, ten years ago the northwest (upper left) area of the park consisted of the realm "Bear Country" which was dedicated to simulated amusements representing country and western culture of the "Hee Haw" variety. Market studies revealed that this area was the least favored by park visitors. It is now gone and replaced by Toontown. Despite this change, and the periodic replacement or addition of rides, the classic Disneyland form remains roughly the same. Disneyworld in Orlando, Florida, contains a larger version of this same scheme that is also replicated in EuroDisney and the Disneyland outside Tokyo.

Disneyland versus Daily Life

As already noted, any visitor to a theme park, except those like jungle safaris that involve live animals, must abandon the private auto and experience the environment as a *pedestrian*. This status stands in sharp contrast to the everyday life of being a commuter in an auto- and train-dependent world. The contrast with suburban life is especially graphic. In suburbia the car is a necessity and walking is discouraged by the layout of housing subdivisions that rarely, if ever, offer pedestrian paths. It is not stretching things to say that suburban housing developments are hostile to pedestrians (Langdon 1994). Because most visitors to Disneyland come from the areas outside the central city, their experience of communion with the crowd is a rare occassion. Suburbanites also find a classic *urban* experience of this kind at malls. Lately, as crime levels have risen in the city and lifestyle changes, such as co-cooning, characterize the routines of urban residents, they too seem to enjoy the unfettered, crime-free pedestrian environment of the theme park, if not the mall as well.

First, when high crime threatens enjoyment of public spaces in the city, malls and theme parks are desirable substitutes for the urban experience. It is also for this reason that despite the apparently infinite possibilities open to Las Vegas casino developers for the pursuit of new fantasy themes, they seem to gravitate back toward mega-structures that replicate central city spaces, such as the proposed Paris or New York-themed casinos discussed in the last chapter. People miss the open and free city and the thrill of pedestrian status within the crowd. Some observers have likened this experience to eroticism (Barthes 1986) or to the unabashed joy and freedom of serendipitous encounters (Lefebvre 1974).

Second, Disneyland-style theme parks offer a contrast in the serving and eating of food. At home, in everyday life, food is designed for subsistence and nourishment. Meals are planned and budgeted. Families eat together only when they can all be at dinner the same time, a usually difficult chore given the complexity of everyone's schedules today. At the theme park food is part of the celebration. It is festival or state fair food. People are never far from food; they can buy things to eat any time and at almost any location within the park. They eat snacks while walking—a classic joy of city living. Compare this to the driver of a car on the freeway munching on a noontime fast-food burger or burrito with one hand, with menacing traffic in all the other lanes. In addition, most theme parks offer a cornucopia of food choices, although none of them may be up to either gourmet tastes or acceptable nutritional standards. Along with the expected fast food franchises, themed environments often offer variations of ethnic dining and other exotic treats. Of course, the prices for all this enjoyment are always quite high compared to food outlets outside the park.

Third, experiencing the park also transforms *family relations*. At home the father rules and the mother manages. Adults define the agenda of daily life. Children exist within a social world of parent expectations. At the park things are different, and even reversed. The kids most often define the routine of the park visit. They direct their parents to the attractions they would most like to see. Thus, if the home is adult centered in its structuring of behavior, then the theme park visit is child centered.

Fourth, in our daily lives *entertainment* is strictly defined by the available time we have after work and family chores. Most people do not leave home in the evening during the week, but are found in front of their television sets, if they have the time to watch. Mass media entertainment, in addition, is a spectacle. People sit passively and view commercialized programming or video tapes. Our society even has a name for this behavior—the "couch potato." At the park, in contrast, entertainment is a festival, not a spectacle (Debord 1970; Lefebvre 1971). The urban experience of the crowd is active and constantly surprising. Beyond the rides and amusements, both the park and the people in it are sources of entertainment.

Fifth, *clothing* in everyday life is highly regimented by both fashion rules and institutional norms. Jobs require their own special styles and children in school are slaves to the conformity of their peer's mode of dress. The work uniform is usually constraining for both men and women who have to "dress up" to pursue their respective careers. At the park, dressing is for leisure and play. People appear as tourists. Some even wear stylized merchandise sold at the park, such as funny hats or mouse ears.

Sixth, a visit to a theme park also provides people with the illusion of escaping from the demands of their own *economy*. At home they are hemned in by the realities of capitalism: the need to work, to budget, to save. Everything one desires has a price. At the park, once visitors can afford to purchase the expensive ticket, which runs over $20 at most parks, they experience the *illusion* of cornucopia or a visit to the classic "land of Cockaigne" where everything is "free." Disneyland used to have one charge for entering the park and then a scale of charges for each of its rides. It was no doubt assumed that people would balk at paying one large sum at the start of their experience, and so the ultimate cost of a day at the park was hidden by this pricing mechanism. Over the years, however, public pressure and a different style of marketing prevailed. The fee structure was changed to a single admission at the entrance. This one-time charge is not cheap. A family of four can expect to pay over $100 at the gate. This expense seems not to deter the average American family, judging by the unparalleled yearly customer levels for Disneyland and Disneyworld, and it does have the added merit for park officials of keeping the poor out.

Finally, the park experience involves a nonquotidian encounter with *architecture*. Here the built environment itself, as with other themed milieus, is a form of entertainment. Each structure provides its own fantasy. The park itself is architecture that entertains. At home, in contrast, places of work lack symbols, as this book seeks to show, and the home stands principally as a sign of status, while lacking the kind of richly endowed themes characteristic of places like Disneyland.

In sum, theme parks are fun. They entertain. In addition, they provide visitors with definite and enjoyable contrasts to their daily lives. Much of this experience is the result of re-creating an urban-style environment in a safe and nonthreatening but also very commercial atmosphere. The theme park as developed by Disney and others also offers people sharp contrasts with the constraints, regimentation, and normative burdens of their everyday existence. A park visit is a holiday from the daily responsibilities of adulthood. Children lead the way, all rides are free, usually forbidden fast foods are the normal mode of nourishment, and even mouse ears can be worn without suspicious reactions from others.

On balance, I believe Disneyland has succeeded not so much because it re-creates the experience of youth alone, nor because it materializes the myths of American society or fantasies, but largely because it liberates people from the constraints of everyday life—especially life that still yearns for the freedom and serendipitious possibilities of urban culture (see Cohen and Taylor 1992). It is this latter feature coupled with the holiday, nonquotidian aspects of food, clothing, and leisure, which makes the park so successful and has led to its conscious imitation countless times in the production of other themed parks across the country.

Beyond the Disney Experience

Much attention has been paid to the Disney themed environments, and rightly so. Many of its critics consider the Disney Corporation as the perfecter of theme parks, which they then fault for being the products of Hollywood glitz and corporate profit-making mentalities. This fits in with a critical, elite perspective that finds only consumer manipulation behind themed facades and only corporate greed behind the proliferation of themed environments (Sorkin 1992). This view is largely true, but, like other reductionist criticisms of American culture, it is only partially true. As we have seen in previous discussions, there are many elements that converge to create an emphasis on a meaningful environment in daily life. These factors create multileveled experiences and symbolic milieus. Our discussion of Disneyland, in particular, illustrates the way Walt Disney's nostalgic yearning for a lost youth and the intimate scale of midwestern small towns articulated with the goals of a large corporation interested in profit. The latter functions as the needs of producers for the realization of capital and does not enter the public's perception of its own experience. Instead, it is the act of consumption with its connections to fantasy and symbols, and the need for meaning, which characterizes the everyday experience of themed environments.

The satisfaction of this thematic need works with a more visceral experience also offered by many themed environments, such as Las Vegas casinos, malls and theme parks, namely, the desire for community and pedestrian communion in public spaces, along with what is often a much-needed holiday from the normal routines of everyday life. People seem to crave this street-level intimacy—a need created by the destruction of public space in contemporary society through suburbanization and the terror of urban crime. The fact that this craving is also satisfied through the activities of the same profit-making enterprises that exploit themed environments should not obscure its fundamental role along with the quest for relief from everyday routines. In this sense, while it is a long way in social development from the simple but redolently symbolic Dogon village in Africa to the Mall of America or Disneyland, it is also not a long step at all. It is only an extension of the human need for a material environment that signifies and has meaning.

As a means of amplifying this idea and making the point that not all successful theme parks are the products of "East Coast" or "Hollywood" wheeling and dealing, let us examine the case of country and western singer, Dolly Parton. Her prospering theme park, Dollywood, is located near the small Tennesee mountain town of Pigeon Forge, at the foothills of Smoky Mountain National Park.

Dollywood and the Generalized Need
for Themed Environments

To suggest that the phenomenon of Dollywood is distinct from connections to Hollywood and the "East Coast" corporate mentality, as perhaps implied from the above, is, of course, quite false. Even the name of this theme park is a conscious attempt by Dolly Parton to play off the well-known Hollywood sign as a signifier for her own pet project. In addition, Dollywood management has skillfully imported to the so-called downhome area of Pigeon Forge all the corporate aspects of running a successful theme park perfected by generations of Disneyland-style establishments. The significance of Dollywood is that its success and scale testify to the generalizability of both themed appeals and the techniques of consumer manipulation within structured environments.

As perfected by Disney, the theme park environment is thoroughly transportable to virtually any milieu. When social critics search for mass media and corporate conspiracies behind the phenomenon of themed environments, they miss the more important point regarding the seemingly universal applicability of theme park engineering to a variety of cultural contexts. Even forgetting the historical antecedents, such as urban arcades, world expositions, and state fairs, it is interesting that theme parks seem to have a universal appeal. Recently, Dollywood announced its negotiations with Japanese investors for a Dollywood park in Japan, a culture as far removed from the Appalachian symbolic field as one can probably get on this earth. Apparently, inspiration for meaningful milieus derives increasingly from the canned culture of Hollywood, popular music, and television.

The theme park, Dollywood, consists of 400 acres with 93 of those developed as of 1994. Originally it was not owned by Dolly Parton. It was called Silver Dollar City and featured Smoky Mountain or Appalachian crafts within a predominently undeveloped park area. In the 1980s, Parton teamed up with Jack Herschend, the owner of Silver Dollar City, lending her name to a new venture that would develop the park. Because Pigeon Forge is close to her birthplace, Parton was very familiar with the area and had many relatives still living there. Besides her name, she, like Walt Disney, brought a personal vision to the proposed theme. Parton sought to enshrine her own rags-to-riches story, from a small town Appalachian girl born into poverty (her father was a poor tobacco farmer) to an international celebrity who has successfully made the crossover from country and western to popular music. The original focus of the proposed park was the Dolly Parton Museum that features re-creations of her birth home, artifacts from mountain culture, and extensive video, audio, and printed displays from her career. Around this shrine, Parton and her partners created a general theme that articulated with the local Smoky Mountain culture. The park features folksy, down-home, country attractions pumped up by marketing and promotional techniques perfected by the Disney Corporation, including Disney-style regulation of customers—"no litter, no alcohol, no bare feet on young'uns" (*Travel Weekly* July 17, 1986:14).

Pigeon Forge, built on a former Cherokee Indian hunting ground, has a population of only 2,800, but it lies on the route to the Smoky Mountain National Park, the most-visited national park in the country. It is also near the metropolitan area of Knoxville, Tennesee, and other larger towns that have thriving motels due to their proximity to recreational areas. Parton's original Dollywood proposed a 9 acre, $5 million expansion of Silver Dollar City. In a meeting with the local town board and state politicians her new corporation persuaded the city to spend $600,000 and the state $1.6 million in public funds for infrastructure improvements, including street and sewer lines.

Map of Dollywood

The park opened in 1986 with attendance at 10,000 a day. By 1993 the annual number of customers was over 9 million. Original ticket prices in 1986 were $12.95 for adults, and $9.95 for children between four and eleven. Children under four were given free admission. By 1994 the downhome marketing strategy received the following prices: $23.99 for adults, $15.99 for children between three and eleven, under three free and senior citizens were admitted at the "special" price of $20.99. This most recent price structure places Dollywood squarely in the same cost range as Disneyland in Anaheim and Universal Studios in Burbank, California.

Dollywood is still evolving and does not have the defined, timeless structure of Disneyland. It combines typical state fair elements with the features of a fully actualized amusement park. It offers a variety of country-style foods (the number of restaurant and fast food places continues to increase), craft demonstrations, and simulated Appalachian cultural artifacts and scenery. The major draw of the park is Parton's connection to the world of popular music. Big name country stars play in several venues and, lately, Dollywood has been exploiting popular music as well, such as a 1950s "oldies" revival. In 1992 twenty-five top names in country music performed during the summer period. The park's only competitors in the region regarding its music attractions are Branson, Missouri, and Nashville, Tennessee.

Park Structure
The land-use design reflects the Disney influence. Dollywood is divided into 6 realms—Country Fair, Showstreet, Rivertown Junction, Daydream Ridge, The Village, and Craftsmen's Valley. However, these are less physical or symbolically distinct than the spatial divisions of Disneyland. The park resembles an upside down T. The horizontal section contains the bulk of the park. A huge parking lot and entranceway at the left end of the T-bar ticket area opens into the first section of the park, Showstreet. The latter is analogous to the Main Street area of Disneyland, but also contains a theater and the fanciest restaurant in the park. Moving along the T-bar, visitors pass Jukebox Junction that features 1950s and 1960s oldies and Rivertown Junction, the site of the Smoky Mountain Rampage, a water slide. Country Fair and the Village make up the other end of the T-bar. These two realms are close together and feature a variety of small attractions. They are circumscribed by the tracks of the Dollywood Express, a five-mile trip on a coal-burning locomotive train.

The long, perpendicular section of Dollywood consists of Craftsmen's Valley that contains the remnants of the old Silver City Appalachian crafts displays. This area features glassblowing, wood carving, metalsmithing, quilting, a wagon shop, a sawmill, and a doll shop. At a side pocket of the valley is located Daydream Ridge that consists of the Dollywood Celebrity Theater, showcasing musical entertainment, and a second water ride, the Mountain Sidewinder. Dollywood as a whole deploys a redundant theme of the small town or Appalachian mountain village elaborated as Showstreet, Jukebox Junction, Rivertown Junction, the Village and the mountain "holler," Craftsman's Valley. The remaining two sections, Country Fair and Daydream Ridge, are little different from other parts of the park, except that the Ridge is built at an elevation allowing a view of the entire area. Both deploy variations on the country or Appalachian culture motif that, along with the career history of Dolly Parton, is one of the two main organizing themes of the park.

Dollywood possesses several large-scale rides typical of other theme parks. They are, however, limited to water themes, such as the Smoky Mountain Rampage, a wet ride down a simulated "runaway river" on a rubber raft, or the water toboggan ride, the Mountain Sidewinder. Along with other typical ride attractions, the park has a 1923 Dentzel Carousel, located in The Village. Over the years the management has been active in upgrading and altering park attractions, so that the current array will undoubtedly change in the future.

Commercial Aspects

Merchandising in Dollywood has also undergone considerable expansion over the years. Its first restaurant was called "Aunt Granny's," an excellent example of redundant semiotic naming that doubles the message of nurturing. Aunt Granny's featured country cooking, including some of Dolly's very own recipes. Most food places featured beef and pork barbecue, ham and beans, hamburgers and southern fried chicken. More recently, pizza was added to the list of affordable foods and a more upscale restaurant, the Backstage, caters to the increasing numbers of urban cow-people attracted to big name country entertainment. The park now boasts 35 retail stores including several that cater to Dolly's style of dressing. In 1991 the Dollywood Corporation proposed to build a 12,000-square foot exit shop. According to officials of the park, "Nobody will be able to leave the park without going through this shop. We'll have a sampling of merchandise from all the shops in the park here" (O'Brien 1991). Finally, the park management has extended the times of the year that it is open for business. Not just a summer attraction anymore, Dollywood is now open for a Fall crafts festival, a winter carnival or "Smoky Mountain Christmas," and a spring attraction. In 1989 the park underwent a $10 million expansion by constructing the Victorian themed village that is open year-round.

Dollywood is no Disneyland. It lacks the well-developed fantasy worlds of the latter. After all, the park really consists of a prior attraction based on Appalachian home crafts and an overlay of Dolly Parton's personal rise to fame and her connections with the commercial world of country music and Hollywood. Nevertheless, as it expanded and its separate realms evolved into sharper relief, it acquired its own special appeal as a family vacation destination. Dollywood merchandising and advertising synthesized the two distinct codes of Appalachian mountain culture, on the one hand, and glitzy show business signifiers on the other.

Parton never ceases to inject homespun rhetoric in her public announcements of new attractions. After unveiling plans for a new, multimillion dollar expansion called "Music Road," Dolly commented that "I am hoping for a really good tobacco crop to pay for all this" (O'Brien 1992). The business logic of Dollywood, however, is pure corporate Disney. While few patrons of Disneyland derive a meaningful experience from the re-creation of midwestern small town life and the youthful fantasies of boyhood games represented by the Disney universe, Disneyland has proved its ability to continually entertain millions with its blend of simulated environments. No doubt a few customers of Dollywood derive a deep, meaningful experience through contact with its simulations of Appalachian culture. But most are drawn by the hybridizing of country music attractions with the easy availability of ham and beans, barbecued ribs and southern fried chicken—a mix also over-layed by a special appeal from Dolly that she's just "one of the folks" despite her $100 million fortune. Using these elements, Parton's park seems firmly established as a second kind of packaged amusement, after the Disney form, if not also a candidate for export to Japan.

Extensions of Themed Environments

Corporate Extensions

As our discussion of Dollywood shows, theme park technique is highly mo-bile, that is, applicable to a variety of contexts. As a mode for the realization of capital, it is exportable to other countries and cultures that have been ex-posed to our popular culture. Because American mass cultural forms, pro-duced by Hollywood and the rock music industry in particular, can be found around the world, fantasies and simulated environments based on them are universal. Theme parks, unlike malls, restaurants, and other com-mercial ventures, are popular as profit-making enterprises because they do not need to sell a product—only an experience. They are distinct spaces that require a price of admission in their own right. They also market attractions to potential customers and guide visitors through the space by regulating crowd control. The fact that in most cases they are successful in selling mer-chandise and food, makes them powerful moneymakers.

Due to their several successful elements, themed environments have ex-tended into other realms. The languishing Burbank, California, back lots of Universal Studios, for example, were refurbished with rides and a structured, themed experience about the making of movies in the 1970s, then marketed as a theme park. Today this Universal Studios Tour is one of Los Angeles's major attractions and the company has exported its park structure to a second location in Orlando, Florida, near Disneyworld. In 1995 ticket prices for Universal Studios in Florida were $32 for adults and $26 for children ages 3 to 11. Several years ago, a multimillion dollar expansion of Los Angeles's Uni-versal Studios park involved the construction of a simulated urban environ-ment called "City Walk" which, like the proposed city-themed Las Vegas casinos, reproduces a *simulated* version of the city experience under tightly controlled conditions. In these and other cases, it is the city itself that has be-come a theme to be exploited by producers of consumer environments.

Elsewhere in the country other corporations have also turned underuti-lized resources or abandoned factories into theme park developments that require a price of admission. Auto World theme park in Flint, Michigan, un-veiled after manufacturing left the city due to the deindustrialization of the

American auto industry, was a failure. However, other examples have been more successful. The Hershey Corporation in Hershey, Pennsylvania, developed land by its chocolate factory into a large theme park. It contains four roller coasters and the tallest wet slide in the country, along with nearly fifty other amusement rides. In addition, Hershey Park contains an 11-acre zoo and special rides designed for small children. Tickets cost $20.95 for adults and $14.95 for children between the ages of 3 and 8. The beer maker, Anheuser-Busch has developed a theme park concept called Busch Gardens. It is very much like other amusement areas and contains rides, entertainment, and attractions for families. Busch Gardens has locations in Virginia and Florida. Tickets for the latter in 1995 were $30.50 for adults and $25.50 for children ages 3 to 9.

Themed environments are being imported into other commercial ventures as well. Many metropolitan areas of the country have experienced difficulty, for example, in keeping their professional sports teams happy in recent years. To maximize their profits, the owners of teams want larger stadia and more fan attendance. Some cities have responded by creating entertainment complexes that are easy to commute to from the suburbs and are attractive to customers. These resemble mall or theme park milieus built within or adjacent to stadia. Baltimore, for example, redeveloped a sports complex called Camden Yards for its baseball team, the Orioles, which includes entertainment facilities. Recently, New York City proposed that they renovate Yankee Stadium as a "theme park" in order to keep the Yankees happy. According to one report, the complex would come with, stores and restaurants around the complex and with new roads leading to new parking garages at the ball park ... estimates of the project's cost are as high as $600 million, making it the most extensive and expensive strategy for keeping the Yankees in the South Bronx that has yet to be presented (Purdy 1995:B-1).

Representing the Unrepresentable

So far we have discussed themed environments that represent aspects of our culture that are also found elsewhere, such as in the movies, popular music or the familiar signs of food and retail franchising. For Disneyland and Dollywood, success of the park environment is based on the linkage between historical aspects of American culture and the glitzy world of showbusiness. In all cases symbolic motifs are designed to simulate common fantasies, popular conceptions of history, exotic locales, nostalgic glorifications of local culture, or idealized conceptions of lost youth. All of the themed environments based on these sources are simulations—artificially re-created milieus designed, not in the interest of historical or everyday accuracy, but for the purposes of entertainment and commerce. Disneyland's Main Street, for example, is a simulation in cartoony fashion of a small midwestern town's main street; it is *not* a

The National Vietnam War Memorial designed by Maya Lin has become a copied form for representing the unrepresentable in other areas of the country and the world. Photo courtesy of UPI/Bettmann.

real main street. However, real midwestern town main streets still exist and some may even bear a resemblance to the cartoony version.

Recently, as thematic competition has increased in the commercial world of restaurants, fast food franchising, malls, parks and other roadside attractions, several other cultural experiences that are not commercial enterprises have become themed environments. When, for example, a memorial to the veterans of the Vietnam War was proposed in the 1970s, an image was recalled of the typical war memorial that can be found not only in the United States but elsewhere around the world. One or more idealized, muscular and heroically scaled soldiers stand as statues over some dedicated plaque that commemorates a battle, war, or those who have sacrificed their lives for their country. Sometimes, this basic form is abstracted and further articulated by metaphor, as in the classic Hellenic statue, Winged Victory, which stands in the Louvre in Paris and is a monumental figure of a draped, winged woman (her head is missing) brandishing a sword. Or, in another example, the similarly scaled and metaphorically abstracted monumental figure of Mother Russia that stands as the memorial to the battle of Stalingrad.

The Vietnam Memorial in Washington, D.C., designed by an actual refugee from that war, Maya Lin, bears no resemblance to this traditional type. It is a long, relatively low, black marble monolith that wends its way along one border of the reflecting pool mall linking the United States capitol building with the Lincoln Memorial. Inscribed on this stark wall are the names of those Americans who died in Vietnam. Since its unveiling, this memorial has become the most profoundly emotional of all Washington places, eclipsing even the solemn cemetery at Arlington and the themed monuments to our greatest Americans. The Vietnam War Memorial is perhaps the first successful built environment that represents the unrepresentable. It exists as a direct line between the grim reality of too many deaths on the one side and the anguish of military survivors or relatives of the deceased on the other. No image, no picture, no video, no music, no simulation can represent the agony of this war, so the wall represents the unrepresentable.

The Vietnam War Memorial is neither a theme park nor a mall. It does not provide its visitors with the urban-style experience that is at the core of many other themed environments, and does not serve as a link between popular cultural forms, such as Hollywood, and the mundane aspects of everyday life. Yet, the memorial is also one of several themed milieus that seek to recall a human drama that cannot be captured in images, music, or words alone. It has been so successful as an expression of the unrepresentable that its vision has recently been copied in several memorials. During June, 1995 at the 50th anniversary of the Battle of Okinawa, a memorial was unveiled that resembles the one in Washington. The Okinawa memorial consists of several low-lying walls of marble arranged in rows, with the names of the 250,000 soldiers and civilians who were killed or injured in the bloody battle. The land-use design of this memorial invokes the ambiance of the Vietnam wall. In a second example, the German government announced plans in 1995 for the construction of a memorial to the European Jews killed by the Nazis during World War II. The winning design for the memorial consists of a gigantic monolith with the authenticated names of the 4.5 million Jews and Gypsies who were killed in concentration camps. The wall motif, therefore, has become a canonical art form—the principal means of representing unrepresentable and monumental tragedies of recent times.

The National Holocaust Museum, which is located not too far from the site of the Vietnam memorial in Washington, D.C., is another highly successful venture that chose to attempt to represent a horrific event. Built with private funds on publicly dedicated land, the Holocaust Museum is, first, a museum—a repository for artifacts that deal with the Holocaust experience of European Jewry. Its designers, however, have orchestrated the viewing of the museum in a way that makes visceral connections between the Holocaust and the museum experience. Thus, it, too, is a themed environment.

At the entrance to the Holocaust Museum, visitors are given a pass with the number of some unfortunate Jew (or gypsy) interned in the camps. The museum's interior was designed to personalize the experience of the holocaust in other ways—through photographs of well-dressed families, pictures of children, exhibits of articles of clothing, of village settings, home interiors—in short, of the normative everyday life of fellow humans. Other parts of the museum are more intrusive. A section represents the Jewish residents of a particular town decimated by the Nazis. Bare brick walls recall the ovens of Auschwitz. Visitors are guided through these and other mini-environments within the museum. In the end, however, the public confronts the ineffable. The domed roof covers a large vacant space, the empty void left by the destruction of European Jewry. Like the Vietnam memorial, all that is left is to imagine alone the unrepresentable anguish and horror of the transforming experience.

There are other holocaust memorials that have been constructed lately, all of which are themed environments. The Museum of Tolerance in Los Angeles features the Jewish experience but also documents the genocide against the Armenians by the Turks in the 1920s. This museum prides itself on its interactive features. Visitors are instructed and informed by informational displays. At the opposite pole is the Jewish extension to the Berlin Museum (Feireiss 1992; Broadbent 1994), designed by Libeskind, which, like the National Holocaust Museum in Washington, tries to represent the unrepresentable. The center piece of the Berlin museum extension is its division by a blank concrete wall, much like the barrier of the Vietnam memorial, shaped as a lightning bolt that traverses the space. The facade is all that is necessary to invoke the unthinkable events and allow feelings to flow. According to Broadbent, the wall circumscribes a space that uses the simplest form of representation, iconic imagery, to invoke the Jewish presence annihilated by the Nazis.

> Libeskind started with a map of Berlin, that is to say an icon, marking onto it addresses of those Jews he saw as essential to the city's cultural history . . . having plotted their addresses, Libeskind connected these by lines which have an elongated Star of David. Across this space is the lightening flash. . . . Since almost all the Jews were deported from Berlin, their possessions destroyed or looted by the Nazis, there was nothing much Jewish to show in the Museum. The 'void' itself is his major exhibit (Broadbent 1994:2).

Recently, there has been some talk in academic circles about attempts to represent the unrepresentable in contrast to the obsession with thematic simulations and virtual reality re-creations increasingly characteristic of our culture. For example, a national museum on the slavery experience has been suggested. This would no doubt be a worthy project. More mundane examples bring us back to the limitations of art and artists in their attempts to represent the depths of human emotion within the context of some cultural medium. Of course, great art often succeeds. The films of Bergman, the paintings of Van Gogh, or the prose of Marquez—to speak of just a few cases—have successfully captured deeply felt feelings and anguished periods of human history. Yet, the discussions about the limitations of representation have been directed toward issues other than the success of great artists.

Lately, people have been concerned with contemporary events for which their powers of representation and depiction seem to fail. Popular culture and the simulations of malls, theme parks, and the like are criticized because of their superficial, false, and idealized representations of experience. However, most people prefer to be entertained rather than confronted by some awesome tragedy of human experience. Simulations carry us away to the fantasy worlds that individuals crave where they are free to shop, eat fast food, and spend time with friends and family. Despite the less welcome presence of the macabre, and, perhaps, because of all the recent energy that has gone into the creation of themed environments, growing attention to the depiction of the unrepresentable seen inevitable—through art and in national gatherings such as the piecing together of the AIDS quilt on the lawn in front of the White House.

Experiencing
Themed Environments

Themed Environments
and Personal Self-Realization

Recall from Chapter 1 our introduction to the approach of semiotics. Some concepts mentioned then can be used now to explain the personal experience of themed environments. Motific milieus are increasingly used as sign-vehicles for making money by commercial corporations. For individual users the same built space presents itself as a sign-function of some social characteristic. Usually the milieu is a sign of entertainment, shopping, fashion, or the invitation to participate in a structured fantasy. What is deployed as a sign-vehicle by the producers of space, becomes a sign of its function for the users. Families consider the purchase of a ticket for a theme park, no matter how costly, as the price of entertainment and they factor it into budgets when they depart on vacations. For the giant corporations that run them, in contrast, the theme park ticket is one source of profits along with the sale of merchandise and food within their attraction. Consequently, any themed, commercial environment is always at the intersection of enjoyable or desirable personal experience and the corporate activity of money-making. In fact, the themed space exists precisely because of the difficulty of profit realization today.

The difference between the way the owners of themed environments and its users view these built spaces is compounded further by the characteristic of polysemy that penetrates the interpretation of signs. As with any signifying object, the sign means different things to different people. Individuals experience themed places in many ways. A study of how people relate to the milieus I have discussed in previous chapters would need to survey children along with adults, the young and the old, men and women, native born

Americans and foreign tourists, people with families versus couples, and groups along with single individuals. The polysemic array of interpretations for any given themed experience might be quite spectacular. This range of meanings that exists for any signifying object is why semioticians are skeptical about claims for a single, definitive interpretation of a themed milieu—an activity that is increasingly common in academic circles.

Polysemic ranges of interpretation can be understood through the concept of the code. Individuals belonging to localized cultures possess certain overarching codes for interpreting their experiences based on their daily life. When people visit a themed milieu, they draw on the code or codes they know best to interpret that space as enjoyable and meaningful. Successful environments appeal to a variety of codes. Visitors to Dollywood, for example, might find certain aspects of the milieu more entertaining or enjoyable than others. They resonate culturally with specific aspects of the park experience. This occurs because their personal, interpretive codes fit some attractions better than others. Disneyland, for example, as conceived by Walt Disney, offers something attractive to every segment of mainstream America. He succeeded remarkably.

Malls work in the same way. The variety of stores and the variety of goods within stores both connect with the most common consumer codes or lifestyle choices in the population. Their merchandising is controlled by chain store marketing that operates nationwide. Each outlet may appeal to particular segments, but those limitations are chosen very carefully with the mix of other stores within the large malls. Peoples' experience of the mall becomes a selective mode of behavior motivated by resonance with those images and commodities with which they are already familiar through mass market conditioning from television, advertising, magazines, and movies.

All themed environments strive to appeal to the largest possible audience or to an intended market segment. The Hard Rock Cafe aims for the young adult market with its limited menu and its emphasis on decor. Dollywood advertises its simulated "country" roots. Las Vegas casinos repeat tried and true themes from American popular culture, even as they innovate an expanding repertoire with new construction. Because of this wide coverage of average consumer tastes, themed milieus are designed to allow polysemy. Each individual brings unique baggage to interpretation, but every commercial milieu that desires success strives to be relevant to many different kinds of people even if they target a market segment. The great American melting pot, for example, is on display each night—walking on Las Vegas Boulevard.

Individuals also function in society through different roles. Adults spend much of their time as workers; that is one source of identity and self-fulfillment. When they engage in recreation or leisure, they assume a different role, that of consumer. As noted, increasingly it is the activity of consumption that most people turn to for self-realization. The conditioning of mass advertising through television, magazines and other media becomes actualized when people enter the themed, commercial space. Indeed, the latter are extensions of the former. That is, themed, commercial environments and our consumer oriented mass culture are integrated through the structure of consumption. According to Langman, "Although there have been historical antecedents in the distribution of goods, malls cannot be thought of apart from the mass mediated images of television that stimulate and soothe at the same time" (1992:40). A visit to a theme park, a mall, a themed restaurant, or Las Vegas casino, enables people to actualize the consuming or commodity-desiring self that remains latent during the work-a-day world of daily life. This other self has already been created by years of conditioning from advertising and image-driven media. Within commercial spaces the consumer self is triggered by the stimulus of a milieu whose themes are integrated with the larger media culture. Where, exactly, can people actualize the consumer part of the self? Where can they encounter the perfumes, clothes, hats, desires, fantasy obsessions, and images that they have been longing for? Increasingly, the answer is within the quasi-public space, the ersatz urban pedestrian culture of the controlled, manipulated, and thoroughly commercialized themed environment. For this reason these places are increasingly the sites of personal self-realization in our society. We are compelled to visit the mall for shopping or the theme park and casino for a vacation, because it is within these environments, after many years of media conditioning, that we feel most like "ourselves."

The Personal Experience of Themed Environments

Several years ago I was invited to give some talks in Brazil. My first stop was Rio de Janeiro. My hosts arranged for me to stay in a small apartment in the section known as "Ipanema," adjacent to Ipanema Beach. The area was quite lovely. There was a bakery directly across the street from my apartment. On my very first morning in Rio I went there for my breakfast. I did not speak any Portuguese, but felt confident that I could execute the interaction. This bakery was very impressive. It occupied a large space with a huge counter area displaying an incredible variety of baked goods. There were many breads to choose from. All of them had just been baked, because that unmistakable smell of freshly made bread saturated the warm, moist Ipanema morning air.

I stepped up to the counter with full confidence and caught the attention of a clerk, a middle-aged woman. She looked at me with an open, anticipating expression. I pointed to the piece of bread I wanted and took out some Brazilian money. She began to speak rapidly. I could not make sense out of anything she said. I kept staring at her and then pointed again at the bread while waving my money. She spoke again and began gesturing. I assumed she was now getting angry, because of her gestures. Her words fell on my untrained ears, deaf to Portuguese. As she spoke and gestured more violently, the realization grabbed me swiftly that I was not getting any bread that morning at all, at least not from this place. I was now totally tuned out to all the sounds she was making and I began to sketch a mental picture of some nice Brazilian supermarket that I hoped was just down the street with open aisles and shelves filled with prepackaged loaves of bread—the exact kind that I would never, under any circumstances, contemplate buying were I back home in the United States.

Through my busy mental picture making, a waking dream of supermarket bliss, I happened to notice that her gesturing had a focus. All the time that she was talking to me and getting increasingly frustrated, her hand motions seemed always to point in the same direction, namely, directly behind me. When that realization finally penetrated my understanding of the interaction, I turned around immediately and noticed a man in a small booth at the back wall who was smiling at me. Propelled both by the intensity of the woman's gesturing and the pleasant smile of the man, I walked quickly to the booth and then noticed that he was behind a large cash register. The clerk yelled over to us with some necessary information and this cashier repeated the phrase. I still did not understand any Portuguese, but handed him some money. He took what he needed, handed me back some of my money plus some change. He then rang up a sale and handed me a receipt while gesturing that I should return to the counter.

When I turned around with the receipt in my hand I saw the woman clerk's face. It was beaming. She seemed so relaxed, or should I say relieved. She watched my every step, like a mother with a baby learning to walk, as I went back to the counter. There the woman proudly handed me the bread I had wanted wrapped in a paper bag and took the receipt from my hand. A few minutes later I was back in my room drinking coffee and eating the very nice, freshly baked bread.

There are, no doubt, many travelers to places with a different language or customs that have had a similar experience. My interaction almost failed. Were it not for the very hard work of the bakery clerk, I would have left that place to search for an American-style supermarket. The interaction was placed in jeopardy not just because I do not speak Portuguese. Clearly, had I known the language, I could have bought the bread quite easily. A significant part of the transaction, however, involved familiarity with the method of buying bread. In this shop, you go to the cashier first and pay your money, then you get your purchase. This is a reversal of the usual method of buying. My lack of familiarity with this reversed method, probably a practice of all such large bakeries in Ipanema, if not Rio, threatened the completion of the purchase.

Every built environment presents itself to the user as a series of obstacles. These are overcome in two distinct ways. First, language is deployed in sign systems to facilitate use. The latter can be either spoken or written discourse. Most public places have explicit graphic sign systems that guide visitors to their respective destinations and facilitate interaction. An airport, for example, could not function without its intricate sign systems, including the automated and continually updated information monitors listing departures, arrivals, and gate numbers. Mall sign systems mark parking places, entrances, and instructions for finding particular stores. Second, users must have some familiarity with the built environment they visit. Even without knowledge of a specific language, there is some greater understanding of interaction that must come from experience. I was lost in the Ipanema bakery both because I could not understand the language and because I was unfamiliar with the method of negotiating that space. However, I had purchased goods in a store before. I had some competency as a consumer from my past. I knew that, no matter how strange the environment seemed, I needed to pay someone and obtain my purchase from someone, somehow. This basic knowledge and familiarity with the practice of consumer purchasing eventually proved to be the foundation for the success of my transaction. Once through it, furthermore, I could, and did, buy bread there as effortlessly as the other "cariocas" every morning.

Familiarity with the sign systems of a themed environment enables users to select a method for the negotiation of the space and, therefore, the satisfaction of their consumer desires. This condition is basic to the success of any commercial place. Let me illustrate with another Brazilian example. During this visit, again involving food, I needed to find dinner. While a tourist can use a guide book to negotiate the space of a strange city, feeding requires some interaction with the natives and, therefore, can be even more of a problem than sightseeing. I found several restaurants in Ipanema that were typical of places I often visited elsewhere. There were others, like bars, coffee houses, and juice stands that were not so familiar. The need for more open interaction between myself and the staff of such places made them more foreboding. However, I could reconcile myself, like any other tourist, to the thought that once I learned how to use those places (as in the case of the bakery) I could negotiate the interaction at the more intimate dinner spots as well.

On the main street of my section there was another alternative. Some enterprising Brazilian had built a McDonald's franchise. I passed this place every day. It was exactly like any other McDonald's. It had the golden arches, the logo, pictures of hamburgers in the window, and signs advertising the daily specials. I knew, in full confidence, that I could enter that place and negotiate the space successfully, even without understanding a single word of Portuguese. I could go in to the Ipanema McDonald's, thousands of miles from my home, and emerge minutes later with the kind of hamburger, french fries, and soft drink of my choice. Extreme familiarity with negotiating the McDonald's environment in my past coupled with the explicit nature of the McDonald's interior sign system guaranteed a successful purchase. During my entire stay in Ipanema I resisted all temptation to enter this place. It became a measure of my success at negotiating the more unfamiliar Brazilian territory. No matter how hungry I was at any given time, I forced myself not to take the easy way out but to try the more foreign food places in the neighborhood. The fact that this McDonald's was always there provided me with some comfort that I would never have to go hungry. However, I never did go in and use it.

When encountering any experience, our success at interacting requires work (Garfinkel 1967; Livingston 1987). We must read the signs of the environment and interpret them. We must follow the cues given to us by others in interaction and behave normatively. If we fail to understand the signs or respond in expected ways, we call attention to ourselves and jeopardize not only our ability to function in the environment but also our well being in the event that others respond to us as a threat (see Goffman 1959, 1963, 1971, 1974).

Interaction in public environments places a burden on all those involved to work for success in interaction. Part of that effort consists of taking the sensory cues of our experience and sculpting them into a comprehensive form. This kind of work is not self-evident nor is it always successful (Garfinkel 1967; Heritage 1984; Livingston 1987). However, it is an activity that often involves considerable creativity. Take, for example, the case of the woman clerk in the Ipanema bakery. She sweated to make her sale. Only by adding to her spoken language a set of gestures that eventually stimulated me to turn around did she snatch the interaction from the brink of complete failure.

In many ways, visits to foreign lands provide the best examples of the basic work required by all of us in every successful interaction (Cohen and Taylor 1992; MacCannell 1976). The tourist must, above all else, learn the methods of negotiating everyday environments. At home these techniques have long since passed into the unconscious, including being programmed into our bodies so that our ways of moving, walking and talking all seem "natural." Only when we visit a foreign environment do these "taken for granted" gestures become problematic. They then require reexamination as appropriate. Hence we dredge them up from our unconscious and deploy them as a set of repertoires in the negotiation of the new, foreign space. The work of tourism becomes this reexamination, relearning, and creative improvisation of methods for successful interaction. The tourist negotiation of the environment is only an illustration of the kind of work we all must do that is taken for granted in our daily lives.

Recently, the sociologist George Ritzer (1993) published a book called *The McDonaldization of America*. His thesis is that the techniques of successful fast-food restaurants are now dominant in all other commercial and institutional environments. Certainly, I can well wonder at the global reach of McDonald's, since that franchise offered welcome relief in my exotic neighborhood of Ipanema. Ritzer, however, situates the phenomenon of McDonaldization squarely within the mental realm of rational techniques for business organization. In particular he follows Max Weber and argues that the success of fast-food places is owed to their "functional rationality," in particular, their efficiency, predictability, quantity, and control of the product through formal rules and regulations (1993:1).

Ritzer's argument is persuasive, but he misses a very important point. The fast-food outlet works because people are familiar with its method of negotiation. Success is not simply the product of rationality as Ritzer would have it, but the result of learning by consumers of the methods of negotiating that built environment. Having eaten in one McDonald's, often because we learned about the place at a young age, we are now equipped to visit not only McDonald's repeatedly with perfect ease but also any other fast-food outlet of similar environmental construction anywhere on the globe.

Ritzer ignores the importance of people playing successfully the role of the consumer and the work that always must be done in interaction. He focuses only on the rational techniques of production that, to be sure, are one reason for profits, but he ignores the human, interactive side of the experience. Fast-food outlets are successful because they offer an easy solution to the method of purchasing food that depends little on spoken language, on the interpretation of the menu or personal relations with the waitress/waiter, as happens in other restaurants. These and other themed environments, with their overendowed, instructive sign systems are fun places to be because they minimize the work that we need to do for a successful interaction.

For McDonaldization and all other associated processes that are successful modes of commerce, the design of environments remains the key to the realization of profits through sales. In order for customers to do their own work properly, commercial material forms have to provide easy-to-decipher visual or discursive signs and be somewhat familiar to the experience of consumers. These are the dual mechanisms pointed to above that are the basis for learning the methods of negotiating the everyday material environment. Every time we enter a fast-food outlet, a hospital, hotel, theme park, casino, airport, or office building we draw on our past in negotiating built spaces, and we interpret the existing cues of the place's sign system to negotiate a successful encounter. Each of these places requires its own special repertoire of actions from us. When we enter a hotel, for example, we know that we must register and dispose of our bags. These activities require certain behaviors on our part. They also involve the staff of the hotel. Both the customer and the staff must negotiate the space and the personal encounter with some ease for the hotel to be successful.

The more obscure the sign system and the more foreign the experience, the less able we are to use the space in the manner we desire. The work of negotiating the place becomes harder and may become so prohibitive that we exit without accomplishing our intended tasks. We can only invoke the required repertoire for negotiating a space when that environment provides us with minimal cues to its function. The Wal-Mart merchandising stores knew all about this process when they pioneered the placement of an official "greeter" that steered new entrants to the store to their desired destinations. Airports do virtually the same thing, but without a greeter, through an overabundance of easily decipherable, universal signs that direct and inform visitors. Tourists to foreign places do not have the luxury of a greeter, but they can hire a tour guide. They can also enjoy learning how to negotiate new environments. This raising of the unconscious, taken for granted repertoire of managing skills, to a direct, conscious level when visiting a foreign place, can be a good part of the fun of going there. Tourism as entertainment can also be viewed as creative work.

Segregation, Surveillance, and the Disappearance of the Public Sphere

A focus on the personal interactive level in the encounter with themed environments helps us understand the critical link between these spaces and the influence of the larger mass culture on the individual pursuit of self-realization. An exclusive concentration on this "phenomenology" of shopping, however, ignores the ways the larger social context structures the opportunities in society for personal fulfillment. Several of these factors, including the processes of segregation and surveillance, have an impact on themed environments. In addition, the rise of commercial, motific spaces must be considered against the backdrop of the general decline in our society's public sphere—the decline in the available opportunities for a public life.

Segregation

On December 14, 1995, Cynthia Wiggens, a young black, single mother, exited the bus that took her to work every morning. She was employed at the immense, up-scale Walden Galleria Mall in the suburbs adjacent to Buffalo, New York. Cynthia lived in the inner city, like many other working poor African-Americans. She was used to the fact that bus transportation was relatively slow and sporadic, especially during the Buffalo winters. Besides these limitations, however, she was also discriminated against as an inner-city resident. This was so because city buses were not allowed to enter the mall area. Every morning she was discharged by city transportation on a busy, seven-lane highway that she then had to cross before she could get to work. One day she didn't make it. A 10-ton dump truck hit her, and she died soon after. According to an account in *Time* (Barnes 1996:33), "Often during the day, charter buses would pull into the Galleria parking lot and disgorge shoppers from as far away as Canada. But the city bus wasn't allowed on mall property."

In the investigation that followed it was determined, much to the embarrassment of both the mall developers and city officials, that the plan for the immense suburban shopping complex intentionally avoided accommodating city buses, thereby making it difficult for residents of the inner city not only to shop there but also, in the case of Cynthia Wiggens and others, to work there. According to *Time*, such actions amounted to "bus-route discrimination." While not as overt in all cases, it is common for malls to be perceived as aiding the patterns of segregation in our society simply because most of them are in the suburbs. Without proper public transportation, they are unapproachable by the less affluent who do not have cars.

An interactive focus on the phenomenology of environmental experience in consumer spaces, such as in the work of Goffman (1971), can overlook the way these places filter people according to the patterns of class, race, and gender segregation. Class distinctions in malls, for example, are present, although they can operate in subtle ways (Gottdiener 1995). Shops selling similar merchandise are often stratified according to the range of prices. Clothes, shoes, or sportswear can be purchased within a large mall at several alternative stores, each of which carries commodities geared to specific household budgets as well as particular lifestyles or fashions. At a typical galleria the consumer can buy a men's suit, for example, for $150 or $1,500.

Class distinctions based on prices at the mall are reinforced by the symbols and themes of different stores. Some project the idea of a fashionable bargain through sale signs, special discounts and promotions. Others justify higher prices by stressing quality. Often the latter is signified through upscale-sounding product names, such as the "Essex" collection of ties, or the "executive" line of business suits. At other times, designer names and celebrity endorsements are used for the same effect. Department stores will even internalize the variation in stores according to household budget segmentation by offering several different lines of commodities that range in price.

The last observation recalls the discussion in Chapter 4 on market segmentation as the dominant mode of commercial sales. Echoing the thoughts in that chapter, our society not only discriminates against people through class and racial distinctions, but also commodifies that discrimination through diversity according to differences in sales price. Metropolitan areas, for example, are segregated in this fashion and the mechanism for racial and class distinctions operates through the price of housing. While it is unlawful in this country to discriminate against people on the basis of race, class, or gender, prospective buyers or renters of housing can only acquire what they can afford. It is not against the law for builders to develop entire sections of suburbia at a particular and relatively high price without a mix of housing stock. In fact, most community zoning and building codes demand it. Thus, what is against the law in sales, namely, the need to treat every potential buyer with the same common courtesy, is countermanded by the production of products according to affordability, which is within the law. The outcome in a housing market that shelters developments which ignore the need for a mix of pricing is the discrimination and segregation of the population in space by class distinctions.

Theme parks reinforce patterns of segregation in our society in a similar way. Because they can charge admission, they can filter visitors out who cannot afford the experience. Theme parks are not public spaces, they are commercial ventures. It would be against the law to disallow entry to the park on the basis of race or religion, yet it is perfectly within the law to discriminate against anyone who cannot afford the cost of entry. As indicated in Chapter 5, most theme parks, even the "downhome" Dollywood, are quite expensive. A family of four will spend well over $100 just for admission. A holiday visit to Disneyworld is an exciting experience for an average family, but its cost can rival a European vacation of the same duration. On my many visits to Disneyland in Anaheim, California, I rarely saw the same admixture of people belonging to different classes, races, and ethnic groups that were present in any of the downtown city spots, although large numbers of middle class Asian tourists might give someone the impression that the park is a place of diversity.

Our society is segregated by class and race. Part of that pattern is produced by the costs of things and part by the way the housing market operates through inner city and suburban distinctions that have an economic and a social interactive basis for discrimination. The consumers at most themed malls, restaurants and parks reflect those patterns of discrimination. Perhaps the only exception among symbolic milieus to this observation is the experience of Las Vegas. I have described that city as one large themed environment with a new style of urban fabric created by the casino-to-casino contrast. It also appears to be the true workers paradise, once dreamt of by hundreds of Marxist revolutionaries, because so many of its visitors are quite ordinary in their circumstances and because there are bargains everywhere for food, drink, and lodging.

Although not as racially representative of the larger society, in Las Vegas there are always a fair number of black and Hispanic people wandering in and out of casinos along with whites of every conceivable class. Some casinos, such as the Mirage, project an upscale image of sorts and can be relatively costly to stay in, others, like the Palace Station or Sam's Town, are more reasonable in price and cater less to a yuppie crowd than to a population of more modest means. On the strip, however, just about all kinds of people can be found making their way from spectacle to spectacle. Las Vegas cannot make up for the personal cultural deprivation produced by a class and racially segregated society, but it helps fuel the myth propagated by other environments that are indeed discriminatory that we are one indivisible society of equals.

Finally, the experience of the themed environment is filtered through the optic of gender. Most places, for example, reflect the values in the larger society by celebrating machismo and peculiarly male fantasies. Las Vegas casinos often celebrate male modes of entertainment, such as the many "girlie" shows regardless of how disguised they are by conventional signs from show business. Western motifs, too, glorify the pumped-up period of the frontier era. Treasure Island provides a spectacle of warring pirates. Excalibur invokes a simulation of male medievalism.

There are, however, exceptions to this domination by male fantasies. The MGM Grand highlights Dorothy and her visit to Oz, amidst its invocation of the glory days of Hollywood film making. Consequently, it adds something of a feminine touch to the spectacle of machismo everyplace else. Can we also consider, as the gendered fantasies of females, the hunk performers that headline many casino shows? Are the topless chorus lines mainly for the men? Even if not, they engineer women simply as sex objects. More graphically, the backstage, less visible part of Las Vegas—its environment of sleaze, sex, and peep shows—constitutes a male-dominated space that commodifies women in the basest terms. Consequently, male-oriented activities characterize the space of Las Vegas and its rich environmental imaging.

Malls, theme parks, and even restaurants can also be read as gendered spaces. Obviously, the activity of shopping is associated more with women than men. Thus, in contrast to Las Vegas, malls may be spaces dominated by the commercialized fantasies of women. They may negotiate these places in ways that are also different than men. That is, the activity of shopping is structured in terms of gender differences. Just as the MGM Grand may serve as an exception in the realm of casino spaces, there is also a theme park that stands out because of its attention to female desires. As described in the previous chapter, Dollywood derives much of its thematic expression from the life of Dolly Parton, its owner. Her "rags to riches" story, which is highlighted by the park environment, is a narrative representation of female mythology for a society dominated by popular cultural forms.

While some visions and fantasies engineered into themed environments might slight the female point of view, this is not the main point I wish to make. If we consider the mall, for example, from a female perspective, we must account for its apparent gender neutrality. The mall space is designed to get all visitors, young and old, male and female, to spend their time and their money, much the way a Las Vegas casino is set up, but through a different experience. The gender issue of the mall space is not one of alleged discrimination against women, but simply of the difference in the experience between men and women. Every themed environment presents a gendered filter through which people experience the space. A phenomenology of the themed environment must account for this gender difference in experience.

Surveillance

In a recent book on Los Angeles, Mike Davis (1990) has called attention to the increasing use of surveillance and belligerent defensive measures built into the new landscapes of suburbia and malls. At times he sounds like a left-wing hysteric that overstates his case, because there is considerable variation in support for defensive measures, rather than a tight conspiracy of the middle class in a war on the poor. Regardless of the causes, however, the facts are accurate. Individuals and commercial environments have increasingly resorted to a variety of regulatory mechanisms to protect access to their personal or marketable possessions. Not everyone, for example, has a fully equipped car alarm or home security system. But a growing number of people would not own one of these commodities without one.

According to Davis,

> The old liberal paradigm of social control, attempting to balance repression with reform, has long been superseded by a rhetoric of social warfare that calculates the interests of the urban poor and the middle classes as a zero-sum game. In cities like Los Angeles, on the bad edge of postmodernity, one observes an unprecedented tendency to merge urban design, architecture and the police apparatus into a single, comprehensive security effort (1990:224).

Davis discusses the way surveillance and other defensive measures are comprehensively engineered into the built environment of Los Angeles. This often takes the form of architectural features, such as the heavy, wrought iron gate in front of a Frank Gehry–designed public library, or the almost ubiquitous signs fronting affluent suburban homes that advertise an "armed response" to intruders. So convincing is his argument that, from the perspective of this book, it can be said that Los Angeles is an environment whose dominant theme is defense against strangers. The signs of a fortress mentality dominate the area as a grand motif.

Where Davis seems to go off the deep end is in his insistence that this is also a form of class warfare and that fortress architecture is a phenomenon caused by middle-class paranoia about crime. Astoundingly, he ignores how poor people also protect themselves using defensive techniques, such as owning attack dogs and by posting hostile signs advertising defense. Fortress architecture is just as characteristic of less affluent inner city areas, where most stores have iron bars on the windows and surveillance cameras along with occasional armed guards, as it is in the more affluent suburbs.

The fear of crime is not a manifestation of middle class paranoia, as Davis suggests. It is a realistic response of all residents to our increasingly violent cities, especially the poor who are most likely to be crime victims. For example, in the inner city of Philadelphia, in December, 1995, the owners of two food markets were gunned down by teenage intruders, leaving community residents without a nearby source of food shopping. Then, too, it is not just the wealthy who deploy fortress architecture, as Davis would have us believe. When the racially mixed working class neighborhood of Five Oaks, in Dayton, Ohio, was besieged by crime and the drug trade because of its proximity to the downtown, it hired defensive space architect, Oscar Newman, who recommended the immediate construction of gates across most of the streets in the community. The result was a drastic decline in crime and an increase in property values, thereby allowing the neighborhood to regain stability (Collison 1996). Those gates are the kinds of objects Davis exemplifies as aspects of fortress architecture, but they exist in and are used by a modest-income, inner-city community.

Commentators on mall architecture have for many years drawn attention to the principle of "introversion" as a fortress-like characteristic of mall design (Gottdiener 1995). Mall facades are blank affairs. Through a lack of signs they stimulate consumers to traverse the space of the parking lot quickly and enter within. Malls are a form of fortress architecture, but only because their architects wish to discourage loitering outside where consumption cannot take place. Here, as elsewhere, examples can be found that argue for a more general and less conspiratorial view for the deployment of the barricade or defensive architecture theme in urban environments.

The problem with this kind of architecture is the way it ruptures the urban fabric by isolating buildings from both the surrounding landscape and the street. One example, is what Davis calls a "stealth house" (1990:238). This is a business or home that presents blank walls to the street. It consciously avoids an integration with the adjacent buildings and the open commerce of the contiguous area. The Danziger Studio designed by Frank Gehry is one case: "The street frontage of the Danziger was simply a massive gray wall, treated with a rough finish to ensure that it would collect dust from passing traffic and weather into a simulacrum of nearby porn studios and garages"(1990:238). Los Angeles and other areas of the country as well, possess many residential communities that are surrounded by high fences. These are often termed "gate-guarded communities." Visitors must enter through a secured and guarded check point, after clearance from the locals is obtained. Security walls, armed guard posts, and signs advertising gated security help create a theme of fortress living (see Langdon 1994). Davis singles out the "armed response" signs in front of affluent homes as a particularly chilling feature of suburban life. They imply that, in addition to the usual type of security devices such as burglar alarms and wired windows, the area is patrolled by a private police corps. Apparently, when intruders or unwanted visitors trip the appropriate signals, armed guards are dispatched. For Davis this constitutes an "imbrication of the police function into the built environment" (1990:250). By breaking down the distinction between the publicly sponsored police department and the lengths that individual citizens advertise they will go to discourage visits from strangers, the private standing armies further develop the theme of the fortress city or fortified residential space.

Elsewhere, in theme parks and casinos, in themed restaurants and airports, security measures have also been taken, but they operate principally through unobtrusive surveillance techniques that deploy hidden technological wizardry. We may be observed in the most minute detail when visiting a themed environment, such as Disneyworld, but the visitor is made to feel comfortable by the landscape. At the very least, most themed environments encourage us to consume and "enjoy." For cities in decline, by contrast, material forms dedicated to defense combine with environmental sign systems to create a belligerent and threatening milieu—a menacing world of estrangement that militates against the idea of a democratic community as the basis for city life.

The Disappearance of Public Space

There is a second way that the transformation and destruction of community ideals can be illustrated. For several decades observers have lamented the decline of places that allow for free public interaction in our society (Sennett 1977; Meyerowitz 1985; Habermas 1989; Chaney 1993). Analyses call attention to the decline of "public space." By this is meant the space of communion where public interaction occurs, where people can meet others at their leisure, and where free and open discussions can take place. When scholars discuss the concept of a public space, most often they have in mind, as the ideal type, the agora or open marketplace of the classical Greek cities. The idea behind the concept is a place that allows for public interaction, not simply the outside environment of our present cities where people rush to and fro after their own affairs without communion with their fellow citizens.

In an interesting study William H. Whyte (1988) discovered that even in the hustle and bustle of the downtown in a large city (Manhattan), people meet others and talk or "schmooze" whenever the opportunity permits. In

Whyte's study, this may include stopping in the middle of a busy sidewalk or sitting on low concrete walls outside of office buildings. These events are in addition to the more common kinds of public interaction in commercial spaces, including sidewalk cafes and al fresco restaurants, or in public parks. Because of the growth of homeless populations in the inner city that have been redefined as "nuisance" groups, some municipalities have taken to redesigning benches and low walls so that people can no longer sit or lie on them (Whyte 1988; Davis 1990). In such ways, public space is assaulted and diminished by city officials.

The most common complaint regarding the decline of public space concerns the effects of high crime rates. Writers that disparage as hysteria the average person's concerns about crime, such as Davis (1990), who also likes to demonize the middle class as the cause of anticivic attitudes, ignore the overwhelming statistics on urban crime, especially when compared to other societies (Gottdiener 1994). American inner cities are, indeed, unsafe places to live, although within these spaces crime rates still vary according to the economic well being of the neighborhood. Thus, the perception of unsafe cities, which is quite realistic, still masks the fact that affluent residents live in safe sections of cities, while the price of crime is paid by the poorer residents who often are its victims.

People cope with the high rate of urban crime by adjusting their behavior accordingly. This change has had a negative effect on the use of public space. City parks, which were purposely dedicated to the concept of public communion, are now rightly perceived to be unsafe places. Cases like the Central Park jogger (Gottdiener 1994:215) demonstrate the danger of using public space during off hours. If most residents view city streets as increasingly unsafe, urban culture, which is dependent on the open interaction of people in public, also declines.

Although many of the contemporary urban analysts confine their observations to the disappearance of public space and its effects (Sennett 1977; Whyte 1988; Davis 1990), they miss a more fundamental and important idea that has been developed by earlier writers on the subject, namely, the relationship between personal space and public space (see Habermas 1989; Arendt 1958; Marcuse 1964; Lefebvre 1971; O'Neill 1972). The one cannot be isolated from the other.

As O'Neill (1972:20) suggests, for example, all our desires are produced in the private realm of our own making. Within that domain we exercise our personal as well as political-community imagination. A nurturing private space allows for personal growth. It is complemented by a nurturing public space that enables the expression of a political consciousness. Public space, then, allows for self-realization in the community realm.

According to this more sophisticated understanding of the private-public distinction, private space was assaulted by the twin forces of consumerism and the invasion of the mass media at the turn of the century and virtually eradicated. For Marcuse (1964:19), for example, individual opinion and the political consciousness were transformed by exposure to "public opinion," that is, the aggregation of individual ideas by state-directed surveys into a "mass sentiment," through the "invasion of the private household by the togetherness of public opinion; [and the] opening of the bedroom to the media of mass communication," (see also Habermas 1989).

Through this process individual ideas were no longer allowed to percolate in their own time from the street level to political venues and democratic mechanisms for the public expression of sentiments. Instead, democracy, itself, was undercut by the "top down" aggregation of individual responses to surveys that were then marketed by the state and corporation alike as "public opinion." With this change came the objective decline of democratic processes in society. Small wonder that, even during a presidential election, a minority of citizens exercise their right to vote. Public opinion polls and media coverage of election results heavily discourage individuals from leaving their homes or even initiating a political dialogue with their neighbors.

Second, consumerism further undermined our private spaces, thereby changing the way all people interacted with the society. The interior spaces of homes became commodified beginning with the 1920s when households were systematically targeted for consumer goods (see Baudrillard 1968; Gottdiener 1995). While household goods had been offered for sale on a mass basis since the previous century, the 1920s brought a more comprehensive approach. At this time, interior spaces were transformed by ensembles of furnishings that pertained to each room as a whole and by the marketing idea that furnishings should express the same theme (Baudrillard 1968; Gottdiener 1995). Thus, companies marketed dining room sets, bathroom sets, and bedroom sets, with each piece coordinated to the ensemble theme. The idea of thematic conformity within home interiors was further reinforced by popular fashion and architecture magazines. The consummate reflection of this comprehensive approach to interior design came from the German Bauhaus which greatly influenced the production and marketing of household commodities in this country as well as Europe (see Chapter 2).

The total commodification of interior space during the 1920s and 30s constitutes one of the earliest manifestations of fully themed environments. Because this effect occurred within the home, it had a special role in transforming private space to a commodified interior that was less a reflection of personal self-expression and more a testament to current consumer fashion. Private space was eliminated and replaced by the commodified logic of interior design. In the same way, the venues of public space—the marketplace, the park, the city sidewalk—that had for thousands of years nurtured community and political communion, were threatened with competition from commodified public places, such as cafes, restaurants, and bars. Nevertheless, the inner life of the individual, simultaneously personal and public, could still be nurtured—especially in the unevenly developed open spaces of society that were only marginally commodified prior to the 1950s.

After 1950, however, public space as a social resource began to disappear and, unlike the claims of city observers like Davis and Whyte, crime and civic ordinances were not factors. Instead, as earlier observers (Marcuse 1964; Lefebvre 1971; Habermas 1989) noted, new forms of social organization dependent on mass media and suburbanization took their toll on public life through the twin forces of the powerful media with its public opinion polling and the transformation of material space. In suburban developments, for example, the common city center was eradicated in favor of privatized backyards. New places of residential living no longer had public space. Suburbanization also introduced the hegemony of the automobile as the dominant form of transportation. The public space of mass transport also disappeared, except for its continued presence in the inner city and along rail commuter lines.

By the 1970s and 1980s there was little left of a material public space, the fear of crime did the rest. More importantly, since the 1920s all social relations were transformed by the twin processes of commodification and mass media influence. Consequently, both private space and public space, along with the powerful tension produced by the private-public dichotomy, were eradicated from contemporary social processes. In their place are the thoroughly commodified spaces of consumption that now exist everywhere, including within the home. As we have been discussing, these new spaces are also themed environments. They are not "public" because they are owned and controlled as commercial businesses. As noted in this chapter, they allow for personal self-expression only within the constraint of consumer identity. The mall may be the new space of public communion, as some have suggested, but it functions in that capacity only within the very restricted context of consumption. Theme parks may be viewed as a kind of public space only if we forget that many people in our society have already been filtered out of that experience by the price of admission. The crowds that we encounter within themed environments are selectively chosen and highly regulated by the structured, commodified experience of the theme park itself. Primed at home by mass media for self-realization through consumption, people enter the pseudo-public space of the themed environment without either political or social desires, as they may once have in earlier times. They pursue self-fulfillment in these places in the only way allowed, through the realization of the consumer role. This is a far cry from the multidimensional everyday urban life of the past.

Themes,
Societal Fantasies,
and Daily Life

Friends of mine returned recently from a wedding in southern California. The bride and groom were in their forties and had been previously married. Both were successful business people. Before knowing each other, they attended acting classes in the Los Angeles area in pursuit of "personal growth." That is where they met. The wedding was a lavish affair expected of people at that career level. What marked the occasion was not its cost, however, but its explicit use of themes. This couple prepared a wedding celebration and ceremony derived entirely from popular culture sources bereft of any influence from religion or family background. Their affair was scripted, cast, produced, directed, costumed and acted as a Hollywood movie. It had several acts, costume changes, and a small cast of characters.

The first act was a Western fantasy and the couple, dressed in fancy Western garb, rode horses to a musical accompaniment. For the second act, the scenery and costumes switched to medieval Venice and the couple performed a scene from Shakespeare's *Taming of the Shrew*. The third act changed location back to the American southwest. At the end of the performance the wedded pair disappeared while guests were invited to watch a professionally prepared video program entitled "The Making of the Wedding of . . ." that was very much like other pseudo-documentaries on the making of Hollywood films. This TV program format recycled images from the ceremony one more time.

This wedding is remarkable for its ability to convey a highly personal family ceremony without the use of religious and ethnic symbols that have legitimized such occasions for thousands of years. A creative blending of popular cultural motifs with the overarching referent of Hollywood cinema was sufficient. For many years people have been attending family celebrations that involve some contemporary themes along with those deriving from religious or ethnic culture. These motifs are veneered over the solid foundation of signs from the latter realms. The wedding or confirmation ceremony is often an articulation between the old and the new. However, the Hollywood wedding that took place in the summer of 1995 was qualitatively different. It represents a successful ceremony that has abandoned all cultural referents from traditional society.

Perhaps everyone has attended a themed family event of some type. These happenings are not unusual. What is remarkable, however, is the cultural shift to events that derive their symbols solely from contemporary culture. A few people in our society, at least, can strike out on their own with themed celebrations that make no reference to religious, ethnic, or family symbolism. Over the years, our society has accumulated an immense dross of signs from cultural expressions that people now recirculate and repackage for their own purposes. They choose from an overabundance of signifying repertoires. Having been jettisoned as images after their initial use by films, rock stars, television, advertising campaigns, consumer promotions, catalogues, and fashion magazines, commercial signs find their way back into use by people for personal reasons of all kinds. As images, their original meanings no longer matter. Instead, only their material manifestations as signs count. Stripped of their deep-level meanings, the images, as objects, become sign-vehicles for individual and group self-expression. Consequently, new uses and new meanings constantly evolve in our society for the flotsam and jetsam of popular culture symbols drifting our way from movies, television, and other media image factories.

The Themes of Built Environments

Human interaction is always *meaningful*. Since the origins of society, people have related to their environment in a symbolic way besides using it to provide necessities. I contend in this book that image making has moved a step beyond the infusion of meaning within the built environment. Everyday life has been set free from the wellsprings of religious, ethnic, and family signs by the plethora of popular culture symbols that now pervade our environment. The distinction of democratic, industrial society between private and public space has been abandoned in favor of a new relation. Our everyday lives currently occur in thoroughly commodified spaces, whether we are alone or in a place of public communion. The public-private distinction no longer exists.

Francoise Choay (1986) argued that the city under the spell of modernist architecture and planning had become "hyposignificant." By this she meant that, unlike the classical or traditional settlement spaces, modernist cities no longer possessed an overarching theme that organized the symbolic content of the built environment (see Chapter 2). Beyond that outcome, the International-school architecture dominating industrial cities also discouraged the use of signs in the construction of buildings. By the 1950s, design practices of this kind created an urban environment limited in its symbolic scope and restricted to the signs of affluence, capitalism, status (both high and low), religion, and ethnicity. The industrial city extolled progress, technological advancement and the austerity of efficient modernist design.

For the inhabitants of cities, the quest for meaning and the need to endow the built environment with a richly textured symbolic content could not be squelched by hyposignificant architecture and urban planning. Many cities reject modernist architecture as the normative design of building. Themed environments reassert their presence even in the most technologically advanced places. Among all the countries of the world, however, the United States stands alone as uniquely endowed with themed places. Nowhere else can you find such a variety of motific restaurants, amusement spaces, malls, airports, or fast food franchises. Nowhere else are pleasure spaces so heavily invested with symbols as Las Vegas, Disneyland, or professional sporting events. While some lament the superficiality of symbols associated with such environments, many people draw upon their sheer abundance in our society to express meaning in daily life.

Looking back on the previous chapters, it seems remarkable that, despite the wide availability of fantasies produced by the media, only a select number of themes are materialized in space. The environment with the most examples is Las Vegas. Even there, casinos manifest a well-defined range of motifs. The influence of the media is important. Themed environments derive inspiration from Hollywood, the world of high fashion, sports, and the music industry. The same codes structure the restaurant chains of the Hard Rock Cafe and Planet Hollywood. At times these codes articulate with others that are more socially grounded, such as the ubiquitous symbolic markers of high status or affluence.

Status

Bugsy Siegel's Flamingo Hotel on the Las Vegas strip was the first to mix signs of wealth with movie stars and Hollywood glitz. Most popular culture themes, combine media signs with those that derive from the code of social status or affluence in our society. Movies and popular novels are *rarely* about the poor and deal almost exclusively, instead, with the concerns of the upper class. Whether aping, celebrating, or satirizing high status, these symbols are most characteristic in our culture.

Status sign-vehicles were once central to the residential needs of the newly rich around the turn of the century. Their conspicuous consumption symbols defined the suburban mansion and, in turn, established the normative features for the construction of middle class suburban homes that still dominate housing appearance today. Status also defines the fashion industry. Designer logos and expensive sneakers costing over $100 a pair belong to the extensive system of signs that defines appearance in terms of status. This same system also regulates merchandise at the mall. Shops are aligned according to the relative status and prestige they enjoy, although this ranking varies with each social subgroup. In short, because consumption is the dominant activity in our society, signs of status, more than class, structure our symbolic universe and personal expectations.

Tropical Paradise

A second popular motif, after status, is "tropical paradise." Real estate interests in Brazil first defined it as a themed environment when they reconstructed Copacabana Beach in Rio de Janeiro as a tourist mecca during the 1920s. Since then, the aura of "tropical paradise" remains powerful as an escapist fantasy. It can be found as the sign in appeals for tourists ranging from commercial places in Hawaii to the Caribbean to Southeast Asia. Tropical paradise is the organizing sign of several Las Vegas casinos, such as The Tropicana, a name that reverberates the Copacabana itself (also once a famous New York nightclub), or the Rio Hotel and Casino, and can also be found as the sign of commodities ranging from shampoo to candy and juice.

The Wild West

The American "Wild West" is another code that organizes themed environments. Again popular in films and novels today, this motif refuses to die. Its symbols are recycled periodically in various manifestations, including virtual reality arcade games that allow gunfights and barroom brawls. The Western motif is popular in airports and hotels in the Southwest. Merchandising makes use of it in the sale of clothing, men and women's accessories such as cologne, and in home furnishings. Occasionally, this theme is used synonymously for "nature"—the Wild West is a sign of nature. Consider, for example, the film City Slickers that featured city-folk encountering the wide-open spaces of the West as a return to "nature." Las Vegas casinos, before strip development, were once totally expressive of this theme.

Classical Civilization

Classical themes seem to have limited uses in our society. Architecture influenced by Greece or Rome is reserved for powerful social institutions such as colleges, banks, or government buildings. While Las Vegas has casinos using this motif, such as Caesar's Palace, they are not duplicated elsewhere. In fact, the Luxor, an Egyptian-themed hotel and casino in the shape of a pyramid, has not been very successful. University campuses once constructed buildings almost exclusively in the classical style. Today, modern and postmodern design prevails. Despite its limited appeal, however, the classical code remains a sign of power. Consequently, it persists as an important symbolic referent in the design of state buildings.

Nostalgia

One popular thematic source is nostalgia, especially the signs of American culture from the 1920s to the 1950s. A common restaurant type is the newly constructed diner using a decor recalling the 1950s. The chain Ruby Tuesday's features an interior that is an implosion of signs from several decades. Some popular television shows also are inspired by an idealized sense of the past recycled in various forms. Nostalgia permeates the personalized visions of both Walt Disney and Dolly Parton and has left its mark on their theme parks. The past is recycled in great simulated heaps by the theme park experience, as it also is in Hollywood films, fashion, and advertising. Part of the allure of historical monuments also relies on the idealized sign of nostalgia. Each of these elements—theme parks, monuments, historical sites, and folk museums serve up a vision of American history consumed by eager tourists. We rediscover our history not through books or college courses, but from visits to themed environments that simulate the past.

The Arabian Fantasy

A sixth theme, one used in a limited way today, is the Arabian fantasy motif. At one time, it was very popular among Las Vegas casinos with names like Aladdin, The Sands, The Dunes, and The Sahara, perhaps because of the desert setting. Lately, its sign value has declined, especially as the entire southwestern tier of the United States has become thoroughly urbanized. Also events like the Gulf War and the continuing tensions and terrorism in the Middle East deflate the caché of "Arabian" symbols. However, this motif can occasionally be found in other areas of the world (outside the Middle East). Several hotels in Hawaii, for example, have developed an Arabian, or more specifically, a Moroccan theme. When in tropical paradise, a tropical theme is redundant, just as the Arabian motif would also be redundant in Arabia. Commercial enterprises vying for tourist dollars in places that have already been plundered for their sign value are forced to think up new codes to exploit to remain competitive. In the above example, one idealized, exotic locale borrows signs from another across the globe.

The Urban Motif

In our discussions of the important commercial places, such as malls and theme parks, I observed that the themed environment sought to recycle the ambience of the pedestrian city. This urban motif is replicated in many forms and most recently is the basis for several new Las Vegas casinos proposed this year. The idealized street setting that creates a condition of safety for pedestrian crowds is one consistently popular motif. There are personal and commercial reasons for this success. On a commercial level, a built environment capturing urban ambiance is used to sell commodities through a re-creation of the marketplace. This form has been in existence for thousands of years. People may go to a market for one thing, but sellers have always known that through proximity they can maximize their chances of attracting impulse buyers. What once worked in the Greek agora or the Istanbul bazaar, also works in malls and airports.

There are also personal reasons for the popularity of the urban ambiance theme. People crave a public experience. There is a certain attraction to people-watching and a certain eroticism in being watched. Communion with the crowd, even the crowd of strangers, means participation in the larger collectivity of society. Because most Americans live in suburbia, not the central city, and have limited opportunity to experience the anonymous crowd of public space, malls, theme parks, and large themed casinos supply this need. People enjoy these environments in their own right as entertaining spaces. Because the urban-pedestrian theme is replicated in so many different contexts, from Universal Studio's "CityWalk" to theme parks and casinos, people probably derive considerable satisfaction from the crowd milieu. Since most people in our society are suburbanites, the urban ambiance of secured, themed environments satisfies desires of which we may be only dimly aware. Crimes in the city and the uncertainty of encounters that are unwanted in urban society prevent most people from enjoying the large metropolis in the same way, but the craving for the communion of public space remains strong.

The urban ambiance created by malls, airport retailing spaces, theme parks, and new city simulations like "CityWalk," works because they are controlled spaces. Mall police, security forces, video surveillance, and in the case of amusement places the high cost of tickets, filters and controls the crowd. Owners and operators of themed environments devote a costly effort to such measures. Every Las Vegas casino, for example, contains banks of 180-degree high speed cameras in the ceiling. Both plainclothes and uniformed security patrol the corridors of malls. For the most part these spaces are safe, in contrast to the large city where anything can happen. I do not mean to imply, however, that no crimes are committed within themed commercial environments. Recently, for example, Disneyland in Anaheim, California, had a gang-related murder. Muggings and robberies occur anywhere, including malls. However, not only is the level of crime low in the highly surveillanced commercial spaces but the public *perceives* them as safe.

For this and other reasons discussed above, the themed environment is enjoyable. People not only are amused by the attractions of these places, they also derive satisfaction from being within the built space itself. We observed this often in the previous discussions. Las Vegas, for instance, once attracted visitors because of its legalized gambling and tolerance for loose morals. Now tourists flock to the area because they find the entire milieu created by the newly constructed casinos entertaining. Las Vegas has become one big theme park with different attractions on every corner of the Strip.

If the controlled urban ambiance is one core element in the attraction of themed environments, then another is the structure that resembles a state fair. Rural residents have for years enjoyed a kind of urban milieu—the crowds of the state fair. Unlike the city and very much like Disneyland, state fairs feature one attraction after another interspersed with places to eat. This form has entertained millions over the years. Theme parks replicate the urban ambiance *and* the state fair ambiance. So does Las Vegas.

Fortress Architecture and Surveillance

Ironically, an eighth theme is the obverse of the controlled and secured urban environment, namely, the fortress sign systems of the "uncontrolled" city discussed in the last chapter. This sign system consists of defensive architecture and belligerent signs. Some of its components are so subtle and unobtrusive that they do not contribute to the visible theme of defensiveness. Surveillance needs and intruder countermeasures, in particular, articulate with the most advanced technological devices. In other contexts, defensive signs can be so common that they constitute an overarching theme for a particular space.

Security seems a ubiquitous need of all communities in the contemporary metropolis. In cities of the past, this desire might have been met by municipal policing of streets, on a formal level, or, informally, through youth gangs and even the mafia. Today many residents of cities have lost faith in the ability of the police to keep them safe, especially within their own neighborhoods. Clearly the relatively high levels of crime in today's urban areas have contributed to this perception. A second factor in the case of Los Angeles and other, newer sunbelt cities are their relatively low population densities. Street policing works best in compact, dense places like Manhattan, but is less effective, even when patrol cars are used, in the sprawling, heterogeneous metropolitan regions of the Southwest.

Consequently, both architectural constructions and local resident behavior have responded with their own security measures. Fortress buildings, gate-guarded communities, visible signs advertising "neighborhood watch" or "armed response" posted in the front of houses, and other, graphic signs, such as the picture of some viscious dog that is readily purchased in any pet store for hanging on home gates, work together to create a new symbolic texture for the urban landscape. Symbols of defensiveness and truculent counter-attack against strangers or intruders eclipses the inviting neighborhood decor of open streets and accessible buildings once characteristic of the past. Now the sign system of the fortress city provides the symbolic texture of the new urban landscape.

Modernism and Progress

A consistently important theme that pervades many environments is the belief in progress and the superiority of technological improvement over time. Early modernism of the nineteenth century championed these related themes as did the modernist architects of the International School, such as Le Corbusier. The theme of progress was celebrated in world's fairs and in commodity advertisements on TV. This motif remains a potent form of packaging new commodities. People may have their suspicions about the attractiveness of modernist architecture, but they retain their soft spot for merchandise that advertises itself as the "latest" or "new" and they seem to thrive on announcements for the most recent marvels of technology. Successful mall interior spaces, for example, make use of the high tech glitzy style of chrome, neon, and glass that first appeared in the type known as the "Galleria." The galleria is possibly the most popular form of mall. It combines the natural lighting and plentiful small shops of the old nineteenth century arcades with the most modern department store merchandising. Gallerias are pleasant places to shop. In areas with severe winters, like Minneapolis, or stifling summers, like Atlanta, climate controlled, fully enclosed malls are attractive and enjoyable places to visit. Both the high tech decor and the commodities of the stores underscore the emphasis on newness or technologically advanced commercialism.

If theme parks and the new urban fabric of the Las Vegas Strip are combinations of urban pedestrian culture and the rural state fair, then malls combine the same city ambiance with the nineteenth century arcade form. Under skylit glass ceilings, an abundance of small shops stands patiently while customers brought in by the big anchoring department stores make their way through the interior space just as they did in the original Parisian arcade (sans department stores). As in the nineteenth century, these stores were harbingers of modernism, providing potential clients with the shock of the new, the exotic, and the technological marvel. In this sense, the arcade was different from the middle eastern bazaar that functioned as a marketplace for essentials along with the occasional exotic display. Small mall shops, like arcade boutiques of the nineteenth century, thrive on the shock of the new and on the impulse buying of people drawn there for other reasons. The high tech, multistoried gallerias across the country maximize this chance consuming with their diversity and large interior space. Although many people still purchase commodities because they are signs of fashion or sign-vehicles of high status, within the mall space they are also seduced by the technological marvel, the exotic commodity or the product that signifies progress and the future.

Representing the Unrepresentable

Along with the many themes discussed above, we have also considered an emergent system of sign vehicles that attempt to represent the unrepresentable. Conceptualizers of such themed spaces refer to some highly emotional historical event without recourse to simplistic signs or cliché. In this category the most successful form is Maya Lin's "blank wall with names" that is now replicated across the globe. Museum spaces that have always used themes to organize individual shows, have recently been enhanced by socially conscious exhibits that depict monumental events in human history. The Jewish Extension of the Berlin Museum is one example. It pays homage to the cultural accomplishments of Berlin Jews and simultaneously enraps visitors within a space that memorializes their demise at the hands of the Nazis, thereby functioning as a museum exhibit of culture *and* a personal experience. In time people will overuse the "blank wall with names" and create the need for another inspirational means to represent heartrending human events without the clichés of obvious symbolization. Themed environments of this kind may intertextualize through exhibits with other cultural forms, such as novels, films, or computer assisted visual-texts that are already successful at expressing deep emotions. The Museum of Tolerance in Los Angeles, one example, accomplishes this to a partial degree by extending the Holocaust remembrance theme to a generalized experience of the costs of racism and genocide using interactive multimedia.

Societal Domination by Consumption

In the main, however, we do not possess a culture with an expanding repertoire of themed environments, but a recycling of the arcade, the state fair, the world exposition, and the ambiance of the cosmopolitan, pedestrian city. The themes of modernism—progress, technological wizardry, and the "new"—are intertwined with themes of status, nostalgia, and fantasies derived from the most hackneyed examples of Hollywood cinema—ancient civilizations, tropical paradise, the Wild West, "Arabia," "Rio," or "Hawaii"—some fantasized geographical scene of exoticism straight out of the

Saturday matinee. Realization that the indulgence in fantasy environments consists of a limited repertoire that in many ways apes Hollywood cinema is, perhaps, the biggest disappointment of this study. New, projected themes, such as the proposed Las Vegas casinos, persist in drawing on this common repertoire. Simultaneously, we should also realize the importance of its irony. While the society and its social programs function to destroy the central city, nostalgic yearning for the ambiance of urban pedestrian culture continues to grow and define new themed environments.

There may also be another logic at work that limits the variety of fantasy elements used by themed milieus. Nearly all the types discussed above—malls, restaurants, airports, theme parks, casinos, and spectacular places of nature—are constructed and owned by commercial enterprises. The motifs chosen for environments designed and mass marketed for profit are very much like the programs sanctioned by commercial sponsors and owners of television networks. Profit-seeking dictates that they conform to the common denominator of tastes. This is so even with the important role of segmentation that splits markets into several alternate lifestyle choices. Throughout the immense diversity of American popular culture, there remains little variety. The margins of "good taste," of acceptable aesthetic or artistic expression, of color schemes and recreational activities are jealously guarded against straying from the mainstream. The "tropical paradise" theme, for example, borrows from the sultriness of Rio de Janeiro or the density of Hawaiian vegetation, but stops short of the eroticism of Rio's beaches and night life. Inside the "Rio" casino in Las Vegas is a very ordinary gambling hall.

Commercialism and the profit motive carefully control the mall. We find a great variety of goods at stacked and packed multistory "gallerias," but they are sold in stores franchised from some chain. Despite an appearance of diversity, all the stores are vaguely familiar. Every large mall across the country has almost the exact kinds of outlets. I can buy Hickory Farms sausage, Waldenbooks, Foot Locker sneakers, and Mrs. Field's cookies at malls in upstate New York, the Midwest, Colorado, Kansas, the deep south, and California.

The concourse tunnel at O'Hare airport illustrates how concerns about profitability and commercial, corporate control limit the motifs of themed environments (see Chapter 3). It was not by accident that terminal owners turned first to the Disney corporation to construct a familiar environment, because Disney images saturate our culture. Surroundings using well known popular cultural icons are able to amuse and entertain. As this case study showed, the more avant-garde aesthetic tastes of the tunnel's architect were rejected, although the Disney images were never commissioned.

Themed restaurants, like Planet Hollywood or The Hard Rock Cafe, and theme parks, like Dollywood, use motifs and images that are already proven commercial products from the competitive worlds of movie making or popular music. Echoes of Tomorrowland and science exhibits at world expositions going back almost 100 years are found in the high tech glitz of gallerias. Conversely, familiar shopping experiences at the mall make a visit to Disneyland also familiar. As a core activity of the consumer society, advertising paves the way for the popular acceptance of commercial images. Through habits of television watching, popular magazine reading, and fashion, consumers are conditioned to mall environments and theme parks. Recently (August 1, 1995), the Disney Corporation merged with Capital Cities/ABC Inc., creating the largest movie–theme park–TV empire. This corporate move, costing $19 billion is one of many ways that information, media, communications, and entertainment corporations are consolidating their profit-making. According to a newspaper account regarding Disney's future *and ours,*

> Its goods are as much images as products, creating a common world taste that is identifiably American. Music, video, films, theater, books and theme parks are the outposts of this civilization in which malls are the public squares, gated suburbs are the neighborless neighborhoods and computer screens the virtual communities . . . The distinctions between information and entertainment, software and hardware, product and distribution are fading fast anyway (Barber 1995: A-15).

If we seek truly varied entertaining fantasies from our themed environments, we may have to look for relief from sources other than the giant corporations that control our increasingly integrated media-information culture. However, these same corporations and the owners of Las Vegas casinos seem to consistently be one or several steps ahead of consumers in innovating entertaining variations on similar, salable environmental themes.

The Social Context of Themed Environments

As we have seen, therefore, environments not only convey themes that are enjoyable, they also play an important role in the economy. In Chapter 3 we discussed how, in a highly competitive consumer-oriented society, owners of businesses must face the challenge of *realizing* profit from production. Increasingly, they accomplish their desires through the medium of thematic consumption. People purchase images along with goods. Typically, the former is more important than the latter for the decision to buy. During the nineteenth century the realization of capital was effected by better selling arrangements. This effort culminated in the success of the large department store first unveiled in Paris and later copied in the rest of the industrialized West. The department store worked because it facilitated shopping. Supplementing this structural change were limited attempts at the thematic presentation of commodities through window displays and dramatic staging within the interior.

Selling techniques were superseded by marketing as the consumer society evolved. Mass advertising became a major component of profit making, as it still is today. Advertising appeals developed the earliest themes of the consumer society, such as the desire for status or the attraction of mechanical marvels. Progressivism and prestige-envy were complemented by advertising copy that created the persona of the consumer through direct enticements that stimulated the desire for objects. This marketing mix of fantasy themes and appeals to the consuming or desiring self remains most important today for the realization of profit making. Marketing considerations are more important than other components of the production process and now most products are conceived, designed and produced with consumer clusters in mind. The population of our society is split into segments characterized by lifestyle. Products are designed and sold expressly for the active consumer segments among these population clusters. Marketing practices reduce lifestyles to various themes or textual codes that can be mechanically replicated in advertising. Commodities, images, signs, themes, and constructed consumer environments all meld together to ease the rapid sale of products.

Lifestyles are organized by symbols and depend on signs for their social differentiation from each other. But they also have a material correlate because they use objects as sign-vehicles. For all of their emphasis on movies and media images, the Disney Corporation, for example, makes millions off tie-in merchandising, as do other mass entertainment businesses such as professional sports. Beneath the image-driven society we retain a world of ordinary objects produced for sale. Most consumption involves the marketing of these material correlates to the symbolically organized lifestyle clusters. Themed environments physically encapsulate this vast domain of commodities.

Themes work in a second way to aid the economy. As we have seen, business interests use motifs as sign-vehicles to sell their particular location in competition with other places. A specific spot can promote itself through the construction of a themed environment that attracts visitors. Vacation areas are typical examples of this phenomenon. As mentioned, in the 1920s Rio de Janeiro entrepreneurs transformed its fringe area beaches into the first "tropical paradise" tourist area with great success. The same theme has been replicated ever since by other third-world places desiring a tourist industry. During the American past, the Hotel Boulderado was created as a sign-vehicle for Colorado interests to attract visitors *and* investment to the area. By so doing they helped create the theme of "the Wild West," another persistingly popular symbolic appeal (recall the Hollywood wedding discussed above).

Presently, city boosters combine several attractions to compete as a location with other places. These may include a successful sports team, a shopping mecca, an entertainment zone, a renovated historical quarter, richly themed restaurants, and, in Las Vegas, themed casino gambling. All these elements are marketed as signs of location by the extraction of their symbolic value. Advertisers promoting a specific place use images of happy shoppers, spectacular forms of entertainment, couples in romantic or active settings, facades of themed milieus, and exciting vistas of waterfronts, downtown skyscrapers, or other grand city settings. As tourism has increased in importance to local economies, the extent of place marketing has also become more competitive. The city has become the sign-vehicle for the profit-making activities of local capital tied to the tourist, shopper, and spectator markets.

Previously I discussed the melding world of themed environments, mass media, giant entertainment corporations, and the commercial control of consumer fantasies. These aspects comprise an ephemeral, image-driven environment existing in a hyperspace of television programming, communications networks, computer internets, film images, and virtual fantasy simulations. In tandem with this world is a second one of material relations involving the manufacture of common objects from cars to sportwear. Objects that are the correlates or sign-vehicles for the images of consumption are manufactured mainly by cheap labor in third-world settings. Sport teams make millions from logo'd hats, but these image-objects are manufactured in Latin American or Southeast Asian sweatshops. Beyond the worlds of entertainment, fundamental principles of making money, such as the control of labor and the selling of commodities, still decide the success or failure of image-exploiting enterprises. Consequently, the themed environments that we experience as consumer-tourists rest on top of relations of exploitation within a world of manufacturing that includes a political economy of global reach.

Cultural Criticism
and Themed Environments

The immediately preceding section is important because it focuses on the ways commercial themed environments fit into the global capitalist economy. By emphasizing the world of production and how marketing has become problematic in the pursuit of profits, as in Chapter 3, we provide the personal experience of themed environments, discussed in Chapter 6, with its appropriate and illuminating social context.

In the tradition of academic social inquiry there is an approach to culture known as *critical theory*. Its earliest proponents belonged to "the Frankfurt School," because they were associated with the university at Frankfurt, Germany before World War II. Because many Frankfurt schoolers were Jews and/or anti-Nazis, such as Max Horkheimer, Theodore Adorno and Herbert Marcuse, they left Germany and established their critical theory tradition in the United States during the war years.

Critical theorists belonging to the Frankfurt School were particularly hostile to popular culture. They treated it, and rightly so, as a mass-produced product of newly emergent "media industries." That is, unlike high culture, such as classical music, produced selectively by artists, popular culture was considered an industrial product of large corporations interested in profits. For this reason, Frankfurt Schoolers considered popular culture as a *debasement* of "culture," and therefore, of daily life, by capitalism through its reduction of all social activities to the pursuit of profit. As Kellner observes, "Production for profit means that the executives of the culture industries attempt to produce artifacts that will be popular, that will sell, or, in the case of radio and television, that will attract a mass audience. In many cases, this means production of lowest common denominator artifacts that will not offend mass audiences and that will attract a maximum of customers" (1995: 16).

As the previous chapters have argued, themed environments are controlled and commercial spaces designed to stimulate consumption for the realization of profits through mass marketing. In that sense, they are mere extensions of the kinds of social forms critically analyzed by the Frankfurt School. Themed environments display a surprisingly limited range of symbolic motifs because they need to appeal to the largest possible consumer markets. They have also replaced the public space of daily life, characteristic of early cities, with a regulated place of consumer communion that restricts access by privileging its availability to the more affluent members of society. Today themed environments eclipse the role of the open urban fabric as the staging ground for social interaction. As the Frankfurt Schoolers might have heartily observed, the duality of private-public space, which was once the constitutive basis for liberal democracy, has been replaced by the implosion of consumption and public presence.

However, most critics today no longer subscribe to the Frankfurt School thesis regarding the debasement of high culture by popular culture. Now we take a more democratic view that appreciates the singularity of popular culture as an authentic form of symbolic expression. A more recent, but equally critical perspective on popular culture, was articulated in the 1970s in the United Kingdom as the Birmingham School of Cultural Studies. Its members rejected the Frankfurt argument regarding the strict division of popular and high culture, and the debasement of the latter by the former. British cultural studies adopted a critical perspective, much like the Frankfurt School, but combined its insights with those of another European, Antonio Gramsci (1994), who sought to understand during the Fascist regime of Italy, why the working class did not rebel against its own enslavement. This Cultural Studies tradition, and Gramsci before it, was more politically motivated than the Frankfurt School, because it sought to connect culture with social movements militating for change.

According to the Cultural Studies perspective, popular culture was a volatile domain within which the working class expressed its own desires, through support for certain commodities or group activities, and the capitalist class pursued the domination of society through the co-optation of culture's symbolic forms. Popular culture was considered a tool of ruling class domination because it assuaged or diverted class conflict into harmless forms of consumption. Consumer lifestyles, then, were considered essentially as forms of ideology that co-opted everyday beliefs to support the status quo. Television watching, for example, diverted the use of free time from after-hours worker assembly and political discussion to couch-potato leisure in front of the "boob tube." In the Gramscian tradition of British Cultural Studies, class conflict was controlled by the production of a symbolic and meaningful world based on consumerism that propagated ideological messages legitimating the domination of society by the capitalist system, or more basically, that diverted interests into socially useful consumption pursuits of personal self-realization.

The Cultural Studies tradition may sound as if it stressed static functional arguments, especially through its emphasis on the role of ideology as a mechanism of legitimation, but this is a false impression. They followed Gramsci, who was a dialectical thinker. In particular, for every cultural expression that was functionally supportive of the status quo, Gramsci believed that the working class could respond with a countermeasure, or "counter-hegemonic" action. Boycotts of commodities and the debunking of legitimation symbols might be two such examples of resistance. British Cultural Studies, therefore, placed great weight on critical cultural theory, precisely because it could supply the alternative readings that would expose the status quo ideology operating in popular culture. Thus, "A cultural analysis, then, will reveal both the way the dominant ideology is structured into the text and into the reading subject, and those textural features that enable negotiated, resisting, or oppositional readings to be made" (Kellner 1995:37).

A good number of contemporary culture analysts subscribe to the dialectical premise of the Gramscian-British approach. While the Frankfurt School might condemn all television programming in the manner described above, adherents of the cultural studies tradition point to the ways average watchers can mobilize counter-hegemonic readings and inaugurate forms of resistance to thoroughly commodified media institutions (see Fiske 1987). Thus, while themed environments are examples of commercially controlled spaces that restrict personal experience to domains dominated by consumption, they also can be viewed as places that allow for personal self-expression and self-realization through modes of resistance (see Langman 1992; Shields 1992; Davies 1995).

I have little doubt, based on my field experiences with themed environments, that they offer opportunities for creative interaction in space. It is for this reason that I reject the distinction between production and consumption, traceable to the early Frankfurt School, and allow for the Gramscian concept of counter-hegemonic consumer behavior. As argued in Chapters 1 and 6, the act of consumption, itself, possesses the potential for productive creativity. Polysemic themed environments may control crowds, but they cannot orchestrate the *meaning* of the experience. Each individual user of themed, commercial space has the opportunity to pursue a form of self-fulfillment through the creative act of consumption. If these places can be viewed as modes of domination, because of their singular emphasis on the realization of capital, they can also be considered spaces for the exercise of consumer resistance, especially when the ability to enjoy existing public spaces in the metropolitan region is severely curtailed for reasons listed in the last chapter.

Despite these observations, however, many cultural studies scholars seem to go too far in the celebration of counter-hegemonic tendencies (see Fiske 1987). One limitation is the dependency on "readings" as a way of describing the experience of culture. An important argument of this book is that culture today takes the form of *material* environments, not simply texts (see Gottdiener 1995). Both the body and the mind are engaged by commercial spaces. As Doug Kellner (1995) astutely argues, an emphasis on readings alone reduces the experience of culture to the level of personal *interpretation*, rather than the interrogation of action or practice. Resistant readings, as Kellner argues, may *not* be true forms of resistance at all. They often sound, when described by Cultural Studies writers, simply like different textual interpretations, that is, different *opinions* about the significance of cultural forms. From the discussions above it should now be clear that, while polysemy characterizes the free play of meaning in themed environments, commercial spaces anticipate different and even counter-hegemonic readings because their design *allows* for a variety of personal interpretations.

The issue of resistance should be framed according to physical behaviors as well as mental exercises. A counter-hegemonic tendency must appear as a social practice (see Hall and Jefferson 1976). An emphasis on the material forms that articulate with popular culture symbols, as in the present analysis of themed environments, avoids the Cartesianism of cultural criticism that limits itself to textual readings. Within these new spaces of communion, analysts should search for alternate and possibly resistant *behaviors* in the manner of Goffman's studies of public interaction (1963, 1971). Finally, it is also important to remember that any *critical* approach to culture must account for the production process and the place of cultural products in the scheme of capitalist social organization, as the Frankfurt School showed, besides the personal experience of culture by individuals, whether they subscribe to or reject the manner of symbolic appeals to consume.

Now an emergent media-information net existing in hyperspace characterizes society and conditions people to desire commodities. Simultaneously the net links up with the material forms of the themed environment that are the physical spaces for the satisfaction of consumer desires. Both the virtual hyperspace of images and the material places of consumption are the dual components comprising our culture today. The current consumption-dominated, themed economy is tied to the production of desires through information flow and image circulation, on the one hand, and the flow of money from consumers to businesses on the other. Popular culture has become a hybrid of ephemeral electronic networks of communication and place-specific material enterprises for the production and realization of profit. If consumers also find represented in this combined ethernet-material media-scape some version of a personal vision, dream, or fantasy, they do so only through the commodification of all such imaging by the creators of the themed milieus.

In short, as Henri Lefebvre once remarked, "Capitalism has found itself able to attenuate (if not resolve) its internal contradictions for a century, and consequently, in the hundred years since the writing of *Capital*, it has succeeded in achieving 'growth.' We cannot calculate at what price, but we do know the means: by occupying space, by producing a space" (1976:21). Our environment is dominated by the space of consumption-consumer communion which has replaced the public-private duality that was once the cornerstone of the early modernist city and the cradle of local democracy. Our themed environments are only limited substitutes for the kind of rich public spaces that are nurtured in a healthy society with open cities and a strong public sphere of action.

Bibliography

Aglietta, M. 1979. *A Theory of Capitalist Regulation.* London: New Left Books.

Applebome, P. 1995. "Franchise Fever in the Ivory Tower." *New York Times Educational Life Supplement,* 2 April, sec. 4A, p. 16.

Arendt, H. 1958. *The Human Condition.* Chicago: University of Chicago Press.

Banham, R. 1971. *Los Angeles.* New York: Viking Penguin.

Barber, B. 1995. "From Disney World to Disney's World." *New York Times,* 1 August, sec. A, p. 15.

Barnes, E. 1996. "Can't Get There from Here." *Time Magazine,* 19 February, p. 33.

Barthes, R. 1967. *Elements of Semiology.* New York: Hill and Wang.

_____. 1972. *Mythologies.* New York: Hill and Wang.

_____. 1983. *The Fashion System.* New York: Hill and Wang.

_____. 1986. "Semiology and the Urban." pp. 87–98 in M. Gottdiener and A. Lagopoulos, op. cit.

Baudrillard, J. 1968. *Systeme des objets.* Paris: Denoel-Gonthier.

_____. 1975. *The Mirror of Production.* Translated by M. Leven. St. Louis: Telos Press.

_____. 1983. *Simulations.* New York: Semiotext(e)

_____. 1993. *Symbolic Exchange and Death.* Newbury Park, CA: Sage.

Benjamin, W. 1969. *Reflections.* NY: Schoken Books.

Bluestone, B. and B. Harrison 1982. *The Deindustrialization of America.* New York: Basic Books.

Braudel, F. 1973. *Capitalism and Material Life: 1400–1800.* NY: Harper and Row.

Broadbent, G. 1994. "The Semiotics of the Void." unpublished.

Bruegmann, R. 1989. "Art and Life Under the Runways: United's O'Hare Tunnel." *Twenty/One,* Fall, pp. 6–17.

Carney, G., ed, 1995. *Fast Food, Stock Cars and Rock-n-Roll.* Lanham, MD: Rowman and Littlefield.

Carson, T. 1992. "To Disneyland." *Los Angeles Weekly,* 27 March/2 April, pp. 16–28.

Cartensen, L. 1995. "The Burger Kingdom." pp. 119–128 in G. Carney, op. cit.

Chamberlain, J. 1965. *The Roots of Capitalism.* Rev. ed. New York: D. Van Nostrand.

Chaney, D. 1993. *Fictions of Collective Life,* New York: Routledge.

Choay, F. 1986. "Urbanism in Question." pp. 241–258 in Gottdiener and Lagopoulos, op. cit.

Cohen, S. and L. Taylor 1992. *Escape Attempts: The Theory and Practice of Resistance in Everyday Life.* New York: Routledge.

Collison, K. 1996. "Urban Planner Gives Advice on Creating Safer Neighborhoods." *Buffalo News,* 23 March, sec. C, p. 1.

Davies, I. 1995. *Cultural Studies and Beyond*. New York: Routledge.

Davis, M. 1990. *City of Quartz*. London: Verso.

Davis, Susan 1992. "Streets Too Dead for Dreamin." *The Nation* 31 August/7 September, pp. 220–221.

Debord, Guy 1970. *Society of the Spectacle*. Detroit: Black and Red.

de Certeau, M. 1984. *The Practice of Everyday Life*. Berkeley: University of California Press.

de Saussure, F. 1966. *Course in General Linguistics*. New York: McGraw-Hill.

Dollywood, Inc. 1995. *Guide Map*. Pigeon Forge, TN.

Eco, U. 1976. *A Theory of Semiotics*. Bloomington: Indiana University Press.

Eliade, M. 1963. *Myth and Reality*. New York: Harper and Row.

Ewen, S. 1976. *Captains of Consciousness*. New York: McGraw-Hill.

Feireiss, K. ed., 1992. *Extension to the Berlin Museum with Jewish Department*. Berlin: Ernst and Sohn.

Fiske, J. 1987. *Television Culture*. London: Methuen.

Fjellman, S. 1992. *Vinyl Leaves: Walt Disney World and America*. Boulder, CO: Westview.

Frisby, D. 1985. *Fragments of Modernity*. Oxford: Polity Press.

Galbraith, J.K. 1978. *The New Industrial State*. Boston: Houghton Mifflin.

Garfinkel, H. 1967. *Studies in Ethnomethodology*. Englewood Cliffs, NJ: Prentice-Hall.

Gergen, K. 1991. *The Saturated Self*. New York: Basic Books.

Geyer, F. ed., 1996. *Alienation, Ethnicity and Postmodernism*. Westport, CT: Greenwood Press.

Goffman, E. 1959. *The Presentation of Self in Everyday Life*. New York: Anchor-Doubleday.

_____. 1963. *Behavior in Public Places*. New York: Free Press.

_____. 1971. *Relations in Public*. New York: Basic Books.

_____. 1974. *Frame Analysis*. Boston: Northeastern University Press.

Goldman, R. 1994. *Reading Ads Socially*. New York: Routledge.

Gottdiener, M. 1986. "Recapturing the Center: A Semiotics of the Shopping Mall." in Gottdiener and Lagopoulos, eds. *The City and the Sign*. New York: Columbia University Press.

_____. 1994. *The Social Production of Urban Space*. 2nd. ed. Austin, TX: University of Texas Press.

_____. 1994b. *The New Urban Sociology*. New York: McGraw-Hill.

_____. 1995. *Postmodern Semiotics*. Oxford: Blackwell.

Gramsci, Antonio. 1994. *Letters From Prison*. Edited by Frank Rosengarten, translated by Ray Rosenthal. New York: Columbia University Press.

Greimas, A. 1966. *Semantique structurale*. Paris: Larousse.

_____. 1976. *Semiotique et science sociales*. Paris: Seuil.

Griaule, M. 1966. *Afrique Noir*. Paris: Musee Guimet.

Habermas, J. 1989. *The Structural Transformation of the Public Sphere*. Cambridge, MA: MIT Press.

Hall, S. and T. Jefferson, eds, 1976. *Resistance Through Rituals*. London: Hutchison.

Harvey, D. 1988. *The Postmodern Condition*. Oxford: Blackwell.

Heller, S. 1994. "Dissecting Disney." *The Chronicle of Higher Education*, 16 February, p. A-1, A-9.

Heritage, J. 1984. *Garfinkel and Ethnomethodology*. Cambridge: Polity Press.

Hervey, S. 1982. *Semiotic Perspectives*. London: Allen and Unwin.

Hoston, J. 1989. *The Modernist City*. Chicago: University of Chicago Press.

Hotel Boulderado. n.d., "Back in Time." Boulder, CO.

Jaguaribe, B. 1991. "The Modernist Epitaph: Brasilia and the Crisis of Contemporary Brazil." Unpublished.

Jakle, J. 1995. "Roadside Restaurants and Place-Product-Packaging." pp. 97–118 in Carney, op. cit.

Jameson, F. 1984. "Postmodernism or the Cultural Logic of Late Capitalism." *New Left Review*, 146:53–92.

Johnson, G. 1995. "It's a Mall World at Airports Nowadays." *Buffalo (N.Y.) News*, January 1, sec. F, p. 2.

Jung, C. G. 1964, ed. *Man and His Symbols*. New York: Dell.

Kellner, D. 1995. *Media Culture*. New York: Routledge.

Knaff, D. 1991. "Shopping Centers Have Become World, Culture of Their Own." *Galleria Supplement, The Riverside (Calif.) Press-Enterprise*, 16 October, p. 4.

Konig, R. 1973. *A la Mode: On the Social Psychology of Fashion*. New York: Seabury Press.

Lagopoulos, A. 1986. "Semiotic Urban Models and Modes of Production." pp. 176–201 in M. Gottdiener and A. Lagopoulos, eds., *The City and the Sign*. New York: Columbia University Press.

Langdon, P. 1994. *A Better Place to Live*. Amherst, MA: University of Massachusetts Press.

Langman, L. 1992. "Neon Cages: Shopping for Subjectivity." pp. 40–82 in R. Shields, op. cit.

Lanza, J. 1993. *Elevator Music*. New York: Picador Press.

Leach, W. 1993. *Land of Desire: Merchants, Power and the Rise of a New American Culture*. New York: Pantheon.

Lefebvre, H. 1971. *Everyday Life in the Modern World*. New York: Harper and Row.

———. 1974. *La Production de l'espace*. Paris: Anthropos.

———. 1976. *The Survival of Capitalism*. London: Allison and Busby.

Livingston, E. 1987. *Making Sense of Ethnomethodology*. London: Routledge.

Loos, A. 1982. *Adolf Loos: Theory and Works*. Translated by C. H. Evans. New York: Rizzoli International.

Lucas, L. 1991. "The Galleria." *Galleria Supplement, The Press-Enterprise*, 16 October, p. 4.

Luckmann, T. 1967. *The Invisible Religion*. NY: Macmillan.

MacCannell, D. 1976. *The Tourist*. NY: Schocken Books.

Mall of America 1992. *Guide*. Minneapolis, Minnesota.

Marcuse, H. 1964. *One Dimensional Man*. Boston: Beacon Press.

Marx, K. (1967 [1868]) *Capital*. NY: New World.

Mayer, T. 1994. *Analytical Marxism*. Newbury Park, CA: Sage.

Meyerowitz, J. 1985. *No Sense of Place*. Oxford: Oxford University Press.

Miller, M. 1981. *The Bon Marche: Bourgeois Culture and the Department Store*. Princeton, NJ: Princeton University Press.

Miller, R. 1990. "Selling *Mrs. Consumer*, Advertising and the Creation of Suburban Socio-Spatial Relations." Unpublished manuscript.

O'Brien, T. 1991. "Dollywood Gets $6 Million Expansion for '92." *Amusement Business* 2 September, 103 (35): 18.

_____. 1992. "New Eatery Fills Niche in Dollywood's Food Service." *Amusement Business* 11 May 104(19):45.

O'Neill, J. 1972. "Public and Private Space." In *Sociology as a Skin Trade*. NY: Harper and Row. pp. 20–40.

Pages of Time, 1951. nd. Millersville, TN: Kardlets.

Peirce, C.S. 1931. *Collected Papers,* edited by P. Weiss and C. Hartshone. Cambridge, MA: Harvard University Press.

Piore, M. and C. Sabel. 1984. *The Second Industrial Divide.* New York: Basic Books.

Postman, N. 1985. *Amusing Ourselves to Death.* New York: Penguin.

Purdy, M. 1995. "Theme Park Atmosphere Part of Proposal for Yankee Stadium." *NY Times,* Wednesday, 25 January, sec. B. p. 1.

Redfield, R. 1947. "The Folk Society." *American Journal of Sociology* 3 (January): 293–308.

Ritzer, G. 1993. *The McDonaldization of America.* Newbury Park, CA: Pine Forge Press.

Rybczynski, W. 1986. *Home, A Short History of an Idea.* New York: Viking Penguin.

Schama, S. 1995. *Landscape and Memory.* New York: Alfred Knopf.

Sennett, R. 1977. *The Fall of Public Man.* New York: Alfred Knopf.

Shickel, R. 1968. *The Disney Version.* New York: Simon and Schuster.

Shields, R. ed., 1992. *Lifestyle Shopping.* New York: Routledge.

Simmel, G. 1957. "On Fashion." *American Journal of Sociology* 62: 541–558.

Smoodin, E. 1994. *Disney Discourse: Producing the Magic Kingdom.* New York: Routledge.

Sorkin, M. 1992. *Variations on a Theme Park.* New York: Hill and Wang.

Stone, G. 1962. "Appearance and the Self." in A. Rose, ed., *Human Behavior and Social Processes,* Boston: Houghton Mifflin. pp. 86–118.

Thomas, B. 1977. *The Walt Disney Biography.* New York: Simon and Schuster.

Travel Weekly 1986, 17 July, vol. 45. p. 14.

Veblen, T. 1899. *The Theory of the Leisure Class.* New York: Macmillan.

Venturi, R., D.S. Brown, S. Izenour, 1972. *Learning from Las Vegas.* Cambridge, MA: MIT Press.

Weber, Max. 1968. *Economy and Society.* edited by G. Roth and C. Witlick. New York: Bedminster Press.

Weiss, M. 1988. *The Clustering of America.* New York: Harper and Row.

Whyte, W.H. 1988. *City: Rediscovering the Center.* New York: Doubleday.

Williams, R. 1973. *The Country and the City.* New York: Oxford.

Williams, Rosalyn. 1982. *Dream Worlds: Mass Consumption in Late 19th Century France.* Berkeley: University of California Press.

Williamson, J. 1978. *Decoding Advertisements.* London: Marion Boyars.

Wright, T. and R. Hutchinson. 1996. "Social-Spatial Reproduction and the Built Environment." *Research in Urban Sociology,* v. 4, New Perspectives in Urban Sociology Series. JAI Press.

About the Book and Author

Mark Gottdiener explores the nature of social change as it has developed since the 1960s as reflected in the "theming" of America, from Graceland to Dollywood, from Las Vegas to Disney World, from the Mall of America to your local mall. Nowhere can modern Americans escape the profusion of recognizable symbols and signs attached to virtually every aspect of their culture constantly reminding them that they are on familiar and comforting grounds. "Just come in, friend, and buy; make yourself at home," these symbols seem to say, thus tying media culture and the seduction of consumerism to the production of ingeniously designed symbolic spaces. This is the first book to explore the origins, nature, and future of themed spaces in our information-overloaded world.

Gottdiener begins with a brief historical account of the shifting importance of themes in the construction of built space. He then evaluates the economic basis for the increasing reliance on symbols in the marketing of commercial enterprises and analyzes contemporary trends in themed restaurants, malls, airports, theme parks, museums, and war memorials. Final chapters are devoted to examining such critical issues as the disappearance of public space, the relation between themes and mass media industries, and the future of symbolic spaces.

Mark Gottdiener is chair and professor of the department of sociology at the University at Buffalo, State University of New York. He has written numerous books including *Postmodern Semiotics: Material Culture and the Forms of Postmodern Life*, *The New Urban Sociology*, and *Urban Life in Transition*. Gottdiener lives in East Amherst, New York.

Index